FORD
IN MINIATURE

• Randall Olson •

VELOCE PUBLISHING
THE PUBLISHER OF FINE AUTOMOTIVE BOOKS

Also from Veloce Publishing:

SpeedPro Series
4-Cylinder Engine – How to Blueprint & Build a Short Block for High Performance by Des Hammill
Alfa Romeo DOHC High-Performance Manual by Jim Kartalamakis
Alfa Romeo V6 Engine High-Perfomance Manua by Jim Kartalamakis
BMC 998cc A-Series Engine – How to Power Tune by Des Hammill
The 1275cc A-Series High Performance Manual by Des Hammill
Camshafts – How to Choose & Time them for Maximum Power by Des Hammill
Cylinder Heads – How to Build, Modify & Power Tune Updated & Revised Edition by Peter Burgess
Distributor-type Ignition Systems – How to Build & Power Tune by Des Hammill
Fast Road Car – How to Plan and Build Revised & Updated Colour New Edition by Daniel Stapleton
Ford SOHC 'Pinto' & Sierra Cosworth DOHC Engines – How to Power Tune Updated & Enlarged Edition by Des Hammill
Ford V8 – How to Power Tune Small Block Engines by Des Hammill
Harley-Davidson Evolution Engines – How to Build & Power Tune by Des Hammill
Holley Carburetors – How to Build & Power Tune Revised & Updated Edition by Des Hammill
Jaguar XK Engines – How to Power Tune Revised & Updated Colour Edition by Des Hammill
MG Midget & Austin-Healey Sprite – How to Power Tune Updated & Revised Edition by Daniel Stapleton
MGB 4-Cylinder Engine – How to Power Tune by Peter Burgess
MGB V8 Power – How to Give Your Third, Colour Edition by Roger Williams
MGB, MGC & MGB V8 – How to Improve by Roger Williams
Mini Engines – How to Power Tune on a Small Budget Colour Edition by Des Hammill
Motorsport – Getting Started in by S S Collins
Nitrous Oxide High-Performance Manual by Trevor Langfield
Rover V8 Engines – How to Power Tune by Des Hammill
Sportscar/Kitcar Suspension & Brakes – How to Build & Modify Enlarged & Updated 2nd Edition by Des Hammill
SU Carburettor High-Performance Manual by Des Hammill
Suzuki 4x4 – How to Modify for Serious Off-Road Action by John Richardson
Tiger Avon Sportscar – How to Build Your Own Updated & Revised 2nd Edition by Jim Dudley
TR2, 3 & TR4 – How to Improve by Roger Williams
TR5, 250 & TR6 – How to Improve by Roger Williams
TR7 & TR8, How to Improve by Roger Williams
V8 Engine – How to Build a Short Block for High Performance by Des Hammill
Volkswagen Beetle Suspension, Brakes & Chassis – How to Modify for High Performance by James Hale
Volkswagen Bus Suspension, Brakes & Chassis – How to Modify for High Performance by James Hale
Weber DCOE, & Dellorto DHLA Carburetors – How to Build & Power Tune 3rd Edition by Des Hammill

Those were the days ... Series
Alpine Trials & Rallies 1910-1973 by Martin Pfundner
Austerity Motoring by Malcolm Bobbitt
Brighton National Speed Trials by Tony Gardiner
British Police Cars by Nick Walker
Crystal Palace by S S Collins
Dune Buggy Phenomenon by James Hale
Dune Buggy Phenomenon Volume 2 by James Hale
Motor Racing at Brands Hatch in the Seventies by Chas Parker
Motor Racing at Goodwood in the Sixties by Tony Gardiner
Motor Racing at Oulton Park in the 60s by Peter McFadyen
Three Wheelers by Malcolm Bobbitt

Enthusiast's Restoration Manual Series
Citroën 2CV, How to Restore by Lindsay Porter
Classic Car Body Work, How to Restore by Martin Thaddeus
Classic Cars, How to Paint by Martin Thaddeus
Reliant Regal, How to Restore by Elvis Payne
Triumph TR2/3/3A, How to Restore by Roger Williams
Triumph TR4/4A, How to Restore by Roger Williams
Triumph TR5/250 & 6, How to Restore by Roger Williams
Triumph TR7/8, How to Restore by Roger Williams
Volkswagen Beetle, How to Restore by Jim Tyler
Yamaha FS1-E, How to Restore by John Watts

Essential Buyer's Guide Series
Alfa GT by Keith Booker
Alfa Romeo Spider by Keith Booker
Citroën 2CV by Mark Paxton
Jaguar E-type 3.8 & 4.2 by Peter Crespin
Jaguar E-type V12 by Peter Crespin
MGB by Roger Williams
Porsche 928 by David Hemmings
Triumph TR6 by Roger Williams
VW Beetle by Ken Cservenka and Richard Copping
VW Bus by Ken Cservenka and Richard Copping

Auto-Graphics Series
Fiat & Abarth by Andrea & David Sparrow
Jaguar MkII by Andrea & David Sparrow
Lambretta LI by Andrea & David Sparrow

Rally Giants Series
Ford Escort MkI by Graham Robson
Lancia Stratos by Graham Robson
Subaru Impreza by Graham Robson

General
1½-litre GP Racing 1961-1965 by Mark Whitelock
AC Two-litre Saloons & Buckland Sportscars by Leo Archibald
Alfa Romeo Giulia Coupé GT & GTA by John Tipler
Alfa Tipo 33 by Ed McDonough and Peter Collins
Anatomy of the Works Minis by Brian Moylan
Armstrong-Siddeley by Bill Smith
Autodrome by S S Collins & Gavin Ireland
Automotive A-Z, Lane's Dictionary of Automotive Terms by Keith Lane
Automotive Mascots by David Kay & Lynda Springate
Bahamas Speed Weeks, The by Terry O'Neil
Bentley Continental, Corniche and Azure by Martin Bennett
BMC Competitions Department Secrets by Stuart Turner, Marcus Chambers & Peter Browning
BMW 5-Series by Marc Cranswick
BMW Z-Cars by James Taylor
British 250cc Racing Motorcycles by Chris Pereira
British Cars, The Complete Catalogue of, 1895-1975 by Culshaw & Horrobin
BRM – a mechanic's tale by Richard Salmon
BRM V16 by Karl Ludvigsen
Bugatti Type 40 by Barrie Price
Bugatti 46/50 Updated Edition by Barrie Price
Bugatti T44 by Barrie Price
Bugatti 57 2nd Edition by Barrie Price
Caravans, The Illustrated History 1919-1959 by Andrew Jenkinson
Caravans, The Illustrated History from 1960 by Andrew Jenkinson
Chrysler 300 – America's Most Powerful Car 2nd Edition by Robert Ackerson
Chrysler PT Cruiser by Robert Ackerson
Citroën DS by Malcolm Bobbitt
Classic Car Electrics by Martin Thaddeus
Cobra – The Real Thing! by Trevor Legate
Cortina – Ford's Bestseller by Graham Robson
Coventry Climax Racing Engines by Des Hammill
Daimler SP250 'Dart' by Brian Long
Datsun Fairlady Roadster to 280ZX – The Z-car Story by Brian Long
Dino – The V6 Ferrari by Brian Long
Ducati 750 Bible, The by Ian Falloon
Dune Buggy, Building a – The Essential Manual by Paul Shakespeare
Dune Buggy Files by James Hale
Dune Buggy Handbook by James Hale
Edward Turner: the man behind the motorcycles by Jeff Clew
Fiat & Abarth 124 Spider & Coupé by John Tipler
Fiat & Abarth 500 & 600 2nd edition by Malcolm Bobbitt
Fiats, Great Small by Phil Ward
Ford F100/F150 Pick-up 1948-1996 by Robert Ackerson
Ford F150 1997-2005 by Robert Ackerson
Ford GT – Then and Now by Adrian Streather
Ford GT40 by Trevor Legate
Ford in Miniature by Randall Olson
Ford Model Y by Sam Roberts
Ford Thunderbird by Brian Long
Funky Mopeds by Richard Skelton
GT – The World's Best GT Cars 1953-73 by Sam Dawson
Honda NSX by Brian Long
Jaguar, The Rise of by Barrie Price
Jaguar XJ-S by Brian Long
Jeep CJ by Robert Ackerson
Jeep Wrangler by Robert Ackerson
Karmann-Ghia Coupé & Convertible by Malcolm Bobbitt
Lambretta Bible, The by Pete Davies
Lancia Delta HF Integrale by Werner Blaettel
Land Rover, The Half-Ton Military by Mark Cook
Lea-Francis Story, The by Barrie Price
Lexus Story, The by Brian Long
Lola – The Illustrated History (1957-1977) by John Starkey
Lola – All The Sports Racing & Single-Seater Racing Cars 1978-1997 by John Starkey
Lola T70 – The Racing History & Individual Chassis Record 3rd Edition by John Starkey
Lotus 49 by Michael Oliver
MarketingMobiles, The Wonderful Wacky World of, by James Hale
Mazda MX-5/Miata 1.6 Enthusiast's Workshop Manual by Rod Grainger & Pete Shoemark
Mazda MX-5/Miata 1.8 Enthusiast's Workshop Manual by Rod Grainger & Pete Shoemark
Mazda MX-5 Miata: the book of the world's favourite sportscar by Brian Long
Mazda MX-5 Miata Roadster by Brian Long
MGA by John Price Williams
MGB & MGB GT – Expert Guide (Auto-Doc Series) by Roger Williams
MGB Electrical Systems by Rick Astley
Micro Caravans by Andrew Jenkinson
Microcars at large by Adam Quellan
Mini Cooper – The Real Thing! by John Tipler
Mitsubishi Lancer Evo, the road car & WRC story by Brian Long
Montlhéry, the story of the Paris autodrome by William 'Bill' Boddy
Moto Guzzi Sporting Twins 1971-1993 by Ian Falloon
Motor Racing – Reflections of a Lost Era by Anthony Carter
Motorhomes, The Illustrated History by Andrew Jenkinson
Motorsport in colour, 1950s by Martyn Wainwright
MR2 – Toyota's mid-engined Sports Car by Brian Long
Nissan 300ZX & 350Z – The Z-Car Story by Brian Long
Pass the Theory and Practical Driving Tests by Clive Gibson & Gavin Hoole
Pontiac Firebird by Marc Cranswick
Porsche Boxster by Brian Long
Porsche 356 by Brian Long
Porsche 911 Carrera – The Last of the Evolution by Tony Corlett
Porsche 911R, RS & RSR, 4th Edition by John Starkey
Porsche 911 – The Definitive History 1963-1971 by Brian Long
Porsche 911 – The Definitive History 1971-1977 by Brian Long
Porsche 911 – The Definitive History 1977-1987 by Brian Long
Porsche 911 – The Definitive History 1987-1997 by Brian Long
Porsche 911 – The Definitive History 1997-2004 by Brian Long
Porsche 911SC 'Super Carrera' – The Essential Companion by Adrian Streather
Porsche 914 & 914-6: The Definitive History Of The Road & Competition Cars by Brian Long
Porsche 924 by Brian Long
Porsche 944 by Brian Long
Porsche 993 'King of Porsche' – The Essential Companion by Adrian Streather
Porsche Racing by Brian Long
Porsche Rally History by Laurence Meredith
Porsche: Three generations of genius by Laurence Meredith
RAC Rally Action by Tony Gardiner
Redman, Jim – 6 times world motorcycle champion by Jim Redman
Rolls-Royce Silver Shadow/Bentley T Series Corniche & Camargue Revised & Enlarged Edition by Malcolm Bobbitt
Rolls-Royce Silver Spirit, Silver Spur & Bentley Mulsanne 2nd Edition by Malcolm Bobbitt
Rolls-Royce Silver Wraith, Dawn & Cloud/Bentley MkVI, R & S Series by Martyn Nutland
RX-7 – Mazda's Rotary Engine Sportscar (updated & revised new edition) by Brian Long
Scooters & Microcars by Mike Dann
Singer Story: Cars, Commercial Vehicles, Bicycles & Motorcycles by Kevin Atkinson
SM – Citroën's Maserati-engined Supercar by by Brian Long
Subaru Impreza: the road and WRC story by Brian Long
Taxi! The Story of the 'London' Taxicab by Malcolm Bobbitt
Toyota Celica & Supra by Brian Long
Triumph Motorcycles & the Meriden Factory by Hughie Hancox
Triumph Speed Twin & Thunderbird Bible by Harry Woolridge
Triumph Tiger Cub Bible by Mike Estall
Triumph Trophy Bible by Harry Woolridge
Triumph TR6 by William Kimberley
Unraced by S S Collins
Velocette Motorcycles – MSS to Thruxton Updated & Revised Edition by Rod Burris
Volkswagen Bus Book, The by Malcolm Bobbitt
Volkswagen Bus or Van to Camper, How to Convert by Lindsay Porter
Volkswagens of the World by Simon Glen
VW Beetle Cabriolet by Malcolm Bobbitt
VW Beetle – The Car of the 20th Century by Richard Copping
VW Bus – 40 years of Splitties, Bays & Wedges by Richard Copping
VW Bus, Camper, Van, Pickup by Malcolm Bobbitt
VW Golf: five generations of fun by Richard Copping & Ken Cservenka
VW – The air-cooled era by Richard Copping
Works Minis, The last by Bryan Purves
Works Rally Mechanic by Brian Moylan

www.veloce.co.uk

First published in August 2006 by Veloce Publishing Limited, 33 Trinity Street, Dorchester DT1 1TT, England. Fax 01305 268864/e-mail info@veloce.co.uk/web www.veloce.co.uk or www.velocebooks.com
ISBN 13: 978 1 84584 027 3. ISBN 10: 1 84584 0 27 5. UPC: 6 36847 04027 7.
© Randall Olson and Veloce Publishing 2006. All rights reserved. With the exception of quoting brief passages for the purpose of review, no part of this publication may be recorded, reproduced or transmitted by any means, including photocopying, without the written permission of Veloce Publishing Ltd. Throughout this book logos, model names and designations, etc, have been used for the purposes of identification, illustration and decoration. Such names are the property of the trademark holder as this is not an official publication.
Readers with ideas for automotive books, or books on other transport or related hobby subjects, are invited to write to the editorial director of Veloce Publishing at the above address.
British Library Cataloguing in Publication Data - A catalogue record for this book is available from the British Library. Typesetting, design and page make-up all by Veloce Publishing Ltd on Apple Mac.
Printed in India by Replika.

Contents

Acknowledgements 4

Introduction 6

1 About handbuilt models 8
- The origins of handbuilt models 8
- The market for handbuilt models 8
- Current builders of handbuilt models of Ford Motor Company automobiles 9
- The character of handbuilt models 10
- What goes into making a handbuilt model 11

2 Ford 14
- Summary of major models
  - The '30s 14
  - The '40s 15
  - The '50s 15
  - The '60s 16
- Model-by-model
  - 1930-1938 17
  - 1939-1948 22
  - 1949-1951 33
  - 1952-1956 42
  - 1957-1959 51
  - 1960-1963 61
  - 1964-1969 64

3 Lincoln 69
- Summary of major models
  - The '30s 69
  - The '40s 69
  - The '50s 69
  - The '60s 70
- Model-by-model
  - 1930-1939 70
  - 1940-1948 71
  - 1949-1951 73
  - 1952-1955 75
  - 1956-1957 83
  - 1958-1960 88
  - 1961-1969 89

4 Mercury 91
- Summary of major models
  - The '30s & '40s 91
  - The '50s 91
  - The '60s 92
- Model-by-model
  - 1939-1948 92
  - 1949-1951 93
  - 1952-1956 95
  - 1957-1959 98
  - 1960-1969 101

5 Builders 103
- A&S Modelmakers 104
- Ashton Models 104
- Auto Buff 104
- BBR 104
- Belgium Trucks/Jupiter 104
- Brooklin Models 105
- Collectors' Classics 106
- Conquest Madison 107
- Durham Classics Automotive Miniatures 108
- Enchantment Land Coachbuilders 109
- ECMA/Jeda 43 110
- Frobly 110
- Goldvarg 110
- Heitech 110
- Legendary Motorcars LLC 111
- Marque One 111
- Milestone Miniatures Ltd 111
- Minichamps 111
- Mini Marque '43' & Mini Marque 112
- Motor City USA 113
- Nostalgic Miniatures 114
- Oakland Models 114
- Precision Miniatures 114
- Rextoys 115
- Sun Motor Company 115
- Tin Wizard 116
- Western Models Ltd 116
- Zaugg/Empire Models 116

6 Suppliers 118

Appendix 1 Contact details 120

Appendix 2 Photo credits 121

Index 123

Acknowledgements

MY PASSION FOR AUTOMOBILES WAS KINDLED AS A CHILD. APPARENTLY, WHEN I was a toddler I could correctly name many cars. This lifelong interest has been channeled, of late, into collecting models of automobiles and light trucks. Of course, as my wife would attest, I have chosen a challenging and costly subject for my hobby. I collect 1:43 scale handbuilt models, and, because I do not have limitless finances and time, I have confined my collection to the cars I remember from movies, books, and my youth growing up in Canada; namely 1930s-60s North American models. Which brings me to the reason for this book.

I love reading about and studying these great little replicas, but no publication exists which offers photographs, details and histories combined. So, I set out to correct this. With the help of many people I assembled close to 2000 photographs which, when combined with the necessary text, would produce a book of close to 700 pages. A fellow enthusiast, Rod Ward, who is the editor of *Model Auto Review*, said that I was unlikely to find a publisher who would undertake such a mammoth project. He convinced me to start with a popular automobile maker instead and write a book dedicated to its models, and that is what I have done. *Ford in Miniature* is the first in what I hope will be a series of such books. Thank you, Rod, for your wisdom.

Originating this type of publication consumes much time and energy. Fortunately, I had the help of many great people whose contributions have made the final product better than I could have imagined.

First, I would like to thank David Larsen. One day a couple of years ago, as an outlet for my frustration after being outbid on eBay for handbuilt models by the same person yet again, I e-mailed this person to 'congratulate' him for once again besting me. Since then, Dave and I have corresponded weekly. He is a provider of knowledge and new ideas and has sustained my interest in this project.

A QUARTET OF FORD MOTOR COMPANY SCALE MODELS. CLOCKWISE FROM TOP LEFT: 1957 FAIRLANE AND 1957 MERCURY TURNPIKE CRUISER BY MINI MARQUE '43'; 1957 LINCOLN PREMIERE BY MADISON AND 1957 THUNDERBIRD BY CONQUEST. (AUTHOR COLLECTION)

During a final rush to provide photographs for the book, a few terrific people selflessly battled the technical challenges of providing me with large digital files via the worldwide web. Andrew Thomas, Jerry Rettig, Alex Moskalev, John Arnold, Mike Stephens, Dean Paolucci and Dirk Mathyssen are to be congratulated for their generosity and perseverance in bringing these photos to you, the reader.

Dozens of other enthusiasts with whom I have come into contact have propelled me in this endeavor. Some of these folks, including luminaries Henk van Asten, Bruce Arnold, Dick Browne, Gene Parrill, Julian and Margaret Stewart, and Thomas Woolter, have contributed photos, lists of models, industry contacts, and even articles. My gratitude to you. To my friends on the Forum 43 board at the www.diecast.org, and all those of you who correspond with me, thank you for the knowledge, energy and time you provide to the hobby, and for inspiring me daily. I am grateful for your kindness.

I have had a good relationship with several suppliers who have kept me updated about new models and given excellent service. I have provided their store details later on in the book so that readers may visit them and add to their collections.

There would be no hobby without the builders. These creative and visionary people have generously furnished me with their history, information and photos that I am pleased to be able to share with you. It gives me great pleasure to provide the builders' details in the appendices.

I would be remiss if I did not extend my gratitude to Rod Grainger, Sam Childs and Judith Brooks of Veloce Publishing whose patience and wisdom have made this a better book than I could have envisioned, and who have enabled this publication to find an audience.

THE AUTHOR, RANDALL OLSON, AND HIS HANDBUILT 1:43 SCALE 1953 LINCOLN CAPRI CONVERTIBLE BY MOTOR CITY USA. (AUTHOR COLLECTION)

Finally, I would like to thank my parents, Lucy and Lawrence Olson who nurtured my passion for many things, including cars; my children, Alex and Mike, whose knowledge of history now extends to 20th century motorcars; and my wife, Lindsay who, even though she may not share my love for it, supports my hobby and all that goes with it.

Randall Olson
British Columbia
Canada

Introduction

About the models in this book

THIS BOOK IS FOR PEOPLE WHO LOVE OLD FORDS AND WHO APPRECIATE model cars.

If a person had over $100,000 and a few years of time, it would be possible to assemble a collection of models similar to that displayed here. However, very few people – including myself – have the wherewithal to do this. I have, with the help of a few dozen fellow enthusiasts, gathered photographs and information to create a 'virtual collection' of a significant number of Ford models for readers' enjoyment.

I intend the book to be informative. However, my primary purpose is to create a visual feast, a 'candy store' as it were of colourful replicas of favorite automobiles that came from Dearborn and Windsor. I hope you will visit the candy store often, coming back frequently to see how during the past 35 years or so, the world's best skilled artists and craftspeople have rendered these beautifully accurate replica automobiles.

The models featured in this publication are 1:43rd scale. This has long been regarded as the foundation scale of the toy and collectible model hobby, with the exception of plastic model kits and promotional models that are usually rendered in 1:24th scale. Lately, die-cast model makers – primarily from China – have been producing 1:18th and even 1:16th models that are quite accurate and feature plenty of detail, including engines and opening doors. The range of models these larger replicas cover is still relatively small and confined to convertibles and special interest vehicles, not what Mum and Dad or Grandpa drove.

What makes this book's models so unique is not that they are only 5 inches long but that they are entirely built by hand from resin or white metal.

Known as 'handbuilt models' or just 'handbuilts' these types

1955 FORD CROWN VICTORIA SKYLINER AND 1955 MERCURY SUN VALLEY, BOTH WITH PLEXIGLAS ROOF INSERT, MODELED BY MOTOR CITY USA. (AUTHOR COLLECTION)

of model are quite unlike the die-cast version you can pick up in the toy store for a low price.

Die-cast models are most often produced in the thousands. Handbuilt models (with a few exceptions) typically have a low volume of 10-250 models. Their production, as their name implies, is very labour-intensive. This makes them quite rare, unusual and expensive, often in the $100-300 range.

In this book I profile Ford models from several builders as well as one of the premier custom design specialists who builds models to customer specification. While the models themselves are the real stars, I pay homage to the builders in a later chapter, together with their details, in case you should want to acquire one or more of their creations.

Many of these models are available from a limited number of suppliers. Full contact information for these people is provided in the Appendices.

Readers will note that occasionally I illustrate a model that is not handbuilt but die-cast and thus mass-produced. I do this because in some cases I believe the model, despite its lack of pedigree, to be of high quality and interest and therefore suitable for presentation alongside many of the handmade models. Many die-cast models, especially those made during the last few years, are accurately proportioned and detailed and fit in with any collection of fine models.

Readers will also notice that I use the '$' symbol when I refer to the price of models; simply for convenience and consistency this is intended to mean US dollars. Similarly, since the automobiles modelled are from North America, I use North American terminology for body styles and parts. Weights and measures, where given, are provided primarily in US terms (even though Imperial measures and later, metric were used in Canada where many of the automobiles were manufactured).

Because this book is intended to be a visual candy store, the several hundred model photographs take precedence over words. To provide some structure to your 'visit' I start out with an orientation to the world of handbuilt models, including a summary of how they are made as well as who has made them, what they cost, and where they may generally be obtained.

Following this section are separate chapters for each of the Ford Motor Company's lines, starting with Ford, followed by Lincoln and then Mercury. Each chapter leads with a summary of the major scale models, by decade, followed by a presentation of photographs of these models through the years. After this each of the major builders are listed with anecdotal history and author's

1952 LINCOLN CAPRI, 1951 LINCOLN COSMOPOLITAN, 1955 LINCOLN CAPRI. ALL THREE WERE MODELED BY MOTOR CITY USA. (AUTHOR COLLECTION)

opinions of their products, together with listings of key Ford Motor Company replicas. The appendices have contact details for the builders, plus the world's suppliers and their contact information, and photographic credits.

Now, I invite you to flip the page and enter the fascinating world of handbuilt 1:43 model Ford Motor Company motorcars and light trucks ...

About Handbuilt Models

The origin of handbuilt models

A LITTLE MORE THAN A GENERATION AGO, COLLECTORS OF SCALE MODEL automobiles had just two primary sources for their collections. The first was model kits from makers such as JoHan, AMT, Monogram, MPC, and Revell. Available as assembled or 'built up' models known as promotionals, and more frequently in kit form, they were made from injection-moulded plastic in 1:24th scale. Reasonably priced and very detailed, the quality of the finished product was heavily dependent on the skill of the builder. To this day, these kits remain popular although the promotional vehicles are much less common.

The second source was die-cast toy models from makers such as Corgi, Dinky, Matchbox, Solido, and Vitesse. Essentially toys, these 1:43 scale metal models were fairly accurate and affordable but very common, and tended to be confined to only a few dozen popular automobile subjects.

A growing number of well-heeled and demanding collectors, who wanted authentic-looking and durable, well-constructed models, began to commission builders to assemble models for them and to customize existing models.

Then one day in the early 1970s, Mikansue (an amalgam of Mike and Sue Richardson, the builders' names) came along with a white metal moulded model kit of a 1940 Dodge. Priced at roughly triple that of a plastic kit, the builders also made a built up at an even higher price. These built ups were snapped up by collectors and soon other builders – such as Precision Miniatures, Auto Buff, Auto Replicas, Nostalgic Miniatures, Provence Moulage, and Zaugg – followed suit. Other builders eventually joined the market place; some producing limited runs of a smattering of models and then disappearing, and a few, like Brooklin and Western, enjoying a long and illustrious history.

TOP ROW FROM LEFT TO RIGHT: 1950 CUSTOM CONVERTIBLE; 1950 DELUXE SQUAD CAR; 1950 CUSTOM 4 DOOR SEDAN; 1950 CUSTOM BUSINESS COUPÉ, 1950 CUSTOM 2 DOOR SEDAN WITH FENDER SKIRTS. FRONT ROW FROM LEFT: 1950 COUNTRY SQUIRE STATION WAGON; 1951 CUSTOM CONVERTIBLE; 1951 VICTORIA HARD TOP COUPÉ; 1950 CRESTLINER 2 DOOR SEDAN WITH VINYL ROOF. ALL MODELS ARE FROM MOTOR CITY USA. (AUTHOR COLLECTION)

The market for handbuilt models

During the last decade the handbuilt niche of the scale model world has consolidated significantly, and can be further sub-divided into six groups:

• Race cars. This is a durable market with strong demand. A search on the internet for 'scale model cars' will locate several sites dedicated to competition models, often of Formula One racing vehicles.

• Dream cars. Dedicated to primarily American concept automobiles from Buick's Y Job of 1939 to the last few Big Three

About handbuilt models

auto show cars from the early 1960s such as Chrysler's turbine car, the market for these wonderful models is small and appears to be shrinking.

• Exotics. Ferrari, Maserati, Porsche, even Delage, Panhard, and Delhaye models are coveted by many enthusiasts.

• British, European and Australian. British, French, Italian, Russian, and Swedish models from the 1920s to present day have a wide following and greatly outnumber models of automobiles from any other country, including North America. Australian models from the last 50 years have a smaller audience.

• Modern American. The latest Corvette, 2004 Chrysler 300, 2000 Thunderbird and the 2005 Mustang have re-energized interest in American models, and are being produced by a few die-cast manufacturers and occasionally as a handbuilt.

• Classic American. The subject models of this book from the 1930s to the 1960s have enjoyed much interest, particularly amongst people who experienced these cars firsthand when they occupied the world's highways. However, the number of builders of these models continues to dwindle, leaving only a handful who dedicate their work to this interesting segment of automotive history. The demographics (age and financial wealth) of both collectors and builders, and the improved mass-production techniques and low cost of 1:18th and 1:24th scale die-cast models, suggest that handbuilt 1:43rd scale models will remain a small and exclusive niche for the foreseeable future.

1936 FORD PHAETON HANDMADE IN WHITE METAL FROM MINI MARQUE '43'. (AUTHOR COLLECTION)

1957 MERCURY TURNPIKE CRUISER 2 DOOR HARD TOP COUPÉ. MINI MARQUE '43' MODELS. (AUTHOR COLLECTION)

1949 FORD CUSTOM STATION WAGON CRAFTED IN RESIN FROM KAGER MODELS. (AUTHOR COLLECTION)

Current builders of handbuilt models of Ford Motor Company automobiles

At the time this book went to press, the following companies were producing handbuilt models of Ford Motor Company cars:

• BBR (Italy) still makes street and Pan Americana race versions of the 'Hot Rod' 1952-54 Lincolns. These are finely crafted models priced at over $200 apiece.

• Brooklin Models (UK). Located in Bath, England, Brooklin is the largest producer of handbuilt models. The builder issues five or more different models of American automobiles annually – usually from the 1930-1969 period. In 2005 it issued a 1957 Ranchero and 1963 Falcon along with a 1934 Pierce-Arrow, 1947 Cadillac, 1952 Chrysler, 1954 Hudson and 1939 Mercury. Its models are nicely proportioned and well finished. Replicas that were not particularly detailed to begin with have become more so as the builder has gradually, over the years, added windshield wipers, door handles, and chromed parts for significant moldings and ornamentation. Clear headlight lenses are still omitted and windshield headers are sometimes painted. Still, these are nice models priced at under $100 new.

• Conquest/Madison (USA). A few years ago these premium models disappeared from the scene when their Dutch founder decided to halt production. In 2005, the company changed hands to an American enthusiast who began reissuing models. Made by Scale Model Technical Services aka SMTS of the UK, Conquest and Madison models are very well done at the high end of the price scale; around $235 each. The 1957 Thunderbird is superb.

• Durham Classics (Canada) models are still available at retail outlets despite the company having ceased production. The models are similar to Brooklin (see foregoing description) but are scarcer and more expensive ($110-$150 apiece). Ford models include a 1939 Ford delivery truck and small bus; 1953-55 pickups and panel vans, and 1941 Ford coupés and convertibles.

• Enchantment Land Coachbuilders (USA) is Jerry Rettig, an artisan builder who releases a variety of scale models through direct purchase and eBay auctions. This builder has made several Ford and Lincoln scale models over the past twenty years. Jerry is also the author of a terrific compendium of handbuilt and die-cast 1:43rd scale models entitled *American Wheels: A Reference*.

• Legendary Motorcars (UK) produced a very elaborate 1960 Lincoln Continental and 1969 Mark III, as well as a 1956 Imperial and 1969 Cadillac at $259.

• Milestone Miniatures (UK) distributes a line called Forty-Third Avenue (or 'FTA') that includes the 1936 Ford, 1966 Comet, and 1968 Torino. This company tends to produce at the lower end of the price spectrum ($100–$125) and detailing reflects this. Build quality is consistent. Milestone Miniatures produces models for other companies and has a broad range of British models, especially Jaguar.

Ford in miniature

A TRIO OF 1955 LINCOLN MODELS FROM MOTOR CITY USA. (AUTHOR COLLECTION)

• Minimarque (UK) issues a couple of new, very detailed model runs a year. Priced at $250, attention centers on Hudson and Packard models, although the company does have an extensive history of Ford, when the models were produced under a different owner (Mini Marque '43'). Minimarque plans to issue a 1958 Edsel Citation 4 door hardtop sedan in 2006.

• Motor City USA (USA) is at the pinnacle of the hobby with exquisitely built models in the medium ($100-$185) and premium price ranges ($225-$300). Motor City USA model accuracy and build quality are incomparable. Recent re-issues are the 1955 Mercury and 1955 Lincoln. Since around 2000, the builder has appeared to focus on 1:18th die-cast hot rods, and service cars (ie ambulances and hearses). It has brought out an entirely new model at the rate of one a year, none of which has been Fords.

• Tin Wizard (Germany) issues attractive, moderately detailed and priced (c$125) 1950 Mercury and 60s Thunderbird models in coupé and convertible configurations. Build quality is high and the company is contracted to produce models for other manufacturers. No new American models are expected.

• Western Models Limited (UK) is the supplier of a broad range of models based on American automobiles, including the 1955 Lincoln, 1958 and 1959 Ford, 1959 Edsel, and 1967 Mustang. The company has been in the business for thirty years and issues a few new American models annually. A recent addition to its line-up is the 1948 Lincoln in both 2 and 4 door sedan body styles. Western Models are slightly more detailed than those from Brooklin and are produced in smaller numbers. They are moderately priced at around $150.

Other companies such as K&D (USA) and Toys for Collectors (USA) contract with some of the foregoing manufacturers to produce particular models, such as the well-priced 1966 Cyclone and 1968 Cougar (both at $100-$150).

SMTS (UK) builds many fine models for other companies. It has an American 'Stocker' racecar version of the 1963 Ford Galaxie.

Several builders produce fine 1:43 handbuilt scale models but have not issued any Ford Motor Company replicas. These include AMR (France), ABC (Italy), Bruce Arnold Models (USA), CCC (France), Highway Travelers (USA), JPS (France), Tron (Italy), and Victory (USA).

For all of the model builders I have listed, please check current details on the internet or at the stockists listed in the appendix.

The character of handbuilt models

Like jewellers, violin makers, and sculptors, builders of handbuilts are artists who sometimes work alone or employ small numbers of people with tremendous skill and love to produce these tiny works of art.

Handbuilts may be available as kits but the vast majority are built up by skilled craftspeople with exceptional skills. Look at a handbuilt model and you will immediately notice a number of things.

1955 LINCOLN CAPRI OPEN CONVERTIBLE AND 1953 LINCOLN CAPRI CONVERTIBLE, BOTH HANDBUILT BY MOTOR CITY USA. (AUTHOR COLLECTION)

The weight is usually the first surprise. White metal handbuilts weigh half a pound (250 grams) or more. The next revelation is the precise detail and minute, fragile pieces such as mirrors, windshield wipers, hood mascots and door handles that can come off with clumsy handling. These are not toys! Also, rich, authentically colored paintwork and excellent proportions are the hallmark of today's handbuilt model cars.

Next is the price factor. Handbuilt models tend to cost from $100-$300 brand new. The price reflects the materials (usually 50-100 parts per model), time and skill that goes into the model; most taking several hours to paint, prepare, assemble and finish, not to mention the creation of the molds and brass master patterns.

The last aspect is intangible: Andre-Marie Ruf of French builder AMR, who created several hundred different handbuilt

About handbuilt models

This close-up shows the impressive level of detail in the interior of a handbuilt Motor City USA model, down to the suspended accelerator pedal (an industry first). Consider that the instrument panel is 1½ inches long and less than ⅜ of an inch wide. Semi-gloss paint is used to emulate the look of leather in the sun visors and seat upholstery. Carpeting looks real with the illusion of binding at the seams. (Author collection)

"As with the finest handbuilt model cars, an AMR model is made of diverse pieces and parts. The average number of parts is 90 to 100. There are pieces of casting (white metal), photo-etched parts, lathe-turned pieces, transparent plastic for glazed parts."

A prototypical handbuilt creator, Andre-Marie Ruf estimated that it required from 15 days to 6 months to prepare the master pattern for a handbuilt car model. Ruf broke down the creation process into the following steps:
- Selection of a model and colors.
- Research of documentation, locating, and examining the real car by photographing it from different angles and taking many measurements.
- Drawing at the scale (1:43).
- Once the model is chosen and the required documents found, it's time to sculpt, clean, polish, cast and draw.
- Next, comes the production of the actual parts used in the model.
- Finally the assembly time of each model, approximately 8 to 10 hours excluding paint drying time.

"This 'caricature' of a miniature model brought by man and his hands, is what gives all the value of a handcrafted model. No machine would know how to replicate this. Those who think a handicraft model has imperfections ... I'm convinced that an industrial model is cold because it is too perfect, consequently, without personality." (From a conversation with Marcel Brossi of www.karmodels.com.)

models, put it eloquently when he said: "I'm convinced that the value of a handmade object is closely connected with the manual work. Those who appreciate my work claim to see an interpretation of the real automobile. My goal is to give to the 1:43 scale the same presence that the 1:1 scale has".

What goes into making a handbuilt model

For the description of the complete creation process of a handbuilt model I turned to AMR Models. Its founder, Andre-Marie Ruf (who passed away in 2004), was one of the most prolific modelers in the hobby. AMR's website (www.amr-modelcars.com) is a shrine to the revered master of handbuilts.

Fascinated from an early age by the world of automobiles, in 1975 André-Marie Ruf launched himself as AMR into the world of artisan miniature car fabrication. He was one of the veterans of the French model car scene; collectors the world over know the style he acquired and refined, which is recognized at first glance.

Not to be overlooked is the challenge of building a scale model by hand. John Roberts, well known for his careful and occasionally whimsical customization of Brooklin and Western scale models, works almost entirely with white metal. Here, he comments about a typical handbuilt Woody wagon, in this case, Brooklin Model's 1948 Buick: "The build process on these was a nightmare. The basic shell had the sides, back, and roof section fitted. Great care had to be taken to ensure that everything lined up. If the sides or back were not exact the roof didn't fit. If any

The first, painstaking step in the life of a handbuilt model is for the subject vehicle to be measured and photographed from all angles. Measurements are then converted to 1:43 scale. Having spent considerable time internalizing all aspects of the vehicle, including its proportions and character, the pattern maker is ready to produce a master pattern. A variety of possible techniques and materials are used, depending on the pattern maker's preference. Some carve the model out of wood and others sculpt using wax. Whatever the sculpting material used, a mold or impression of the model and its parts (up to 100) are created and brass is poured into the mold to create a master pattern that can be used repeatedly. The brass master pictured here is for a '56 Mercury hard top. The Argentine builder ultimately did not issue this Goldvarg Collection Model. This photo is an enhanced digital image derived from the Goldvarg Collection product brochure in the author's collection.

Ford in Miniature

Molds are then created around each pattern, ensuring there are no air bubbles, warping, or build-up of excess materials. White metal such as pewter is the most common material, but resin is also used. Here, a technician pours the molten white metal into a mold. Centrifugal (spinning) molding equipment is used to speed the process and improve the quality of the product. (Courtesy Durham Classics Automotive Miniatures)

Final detailing of parts, such as polishing brightwork, is done before assembly. Models are then hand assembled by individuals with exceptionally fine motor skills. (Courtesy Durham Classics Automotive Miniatures)

Castings, such as these 1953 F-100 truck bodies, are meticulously checked, excess flash is removed, and they are prepared for painting. (Courtesy Durham Classics Automotive Miniatures)

Genuine automotive paint is applied, and – in the case of chrome white metal parts such as bumpers – nickel plating is often employed. On the more expensive models, tiny, delicate pieces such as script and wipers employ a photo-etching process where acid is used to burn away superfluous material to create precise, minute 1:43 scale accurate pieces. (Courtesy Durham Classics Automotive Miniatures)

piece wasn't right the vac form [windows] wouldn't fit, and if this was wrong it fouled the seats and creased. Each stage had to be allowed to dry, meaning the model was on the benches for longer than usual.

"A lot were made so it's not rare. This was a good model – take it off your shelf and look at it. The maroon bits are all one casting. The roof is attached to the rest by two thin A posts and two thin C posts. When the bodies were first cast they were breaking up coming out of the molds. Sidebars had to be cast in and then when the shells were cleaned up they had to be removed.

"Most Woodies were designed with three 'wood' sections: two sides and a back. When casting white metal, temperature is critical. Minute variations cause variations in the size of casting. In a one- or two-piece body this can be overcome. A Woody will have four, or even five (the roof) sections. If the temperature was slightly different some pieces may not fit properly, causing extra fettling or melting down and recasting ... all time-consuming. Add to this the spraying of the 'wood' sections which must all match over a two stage process, and the extra effort needed becomes apparent."

Finally, Bruce Arnold, who has made several renowned patterns and is an expert model maker and detailer, had this to say about the character of handbuilt models and their value, both intrinsic and monetary: "Building a high dollar hand-built, while not exactly brain surgery, is not easy. An expert historian must be consulted and hundreds of photographs and measurements must be taken. After all is said and done, the model must face the public. Reviewers who have never even seen the real car take a crack at it, and everyone else is suddenly an 'expert'. There is no virtually no profit margin in this business yet some feel that any model that they can't afford is a bad model.

"This brings up the subject of value. Though many quality

About handbuilt models

1:43 scale models have maintained much of their original investment over the years, models associated with legitimate artisans have dramatically increased in value. A pantographed or computer-generated master has little intrinsic value to automotive fine art collectors. There is, indeed, something almost spiritual about carefully duplicating the same tool strokes over complicated surfaces, and, perhaps, tapping into the same stream of consciousness as the original modeler; in a way, reliving the experience. As the shapes emerge exactly the same, they become a slice of life and time. A machinist sitting at a pantograph cannot accomplish this."

"If your collection is well thought out and, more importantly, accurate in scale and design, it will more than keep pace with a savings account, a discipline which you would probably have never started otherwise. If you can manage to obtain the very best, because of eBay, your collection is already skyrocketing in value and there is no end in sight. If you have hundreds, or thousands, of obsolete mediocre 'toys' that are losing value, it's time to sell, sell, sell!"

Bruce Arnold's candid comments appear underneath some of the photographs in this book.

Why not visit Veloce on the web? – www.velocebooks.com
New book news • Special offers • Details of all books in print • Gift vouchers

FORD 2

As befits this venerable automaker, 1:43rd scale handbuilt replicas of Fords from 1930 to 1960 abound. Selection becomes leaner after 1960, but even then it is still possible to find examples of Thunderbirds, Falcons, Mustangs (of course), and the full-sized Ford and mid-sized Torino from the '60s.

The list of Ford replicas is quite long, so I will just note, by time period, a few of what are, in my opinion, significant models.

Summary of major models — The '30s

For Ford, the thirties really began with the introduction of the Model A. This example is a 1928 by Minichamps; Ford's 1936 top down phaeton by Mini Marque '43'. (Author collection)

The first handbuilt Ford to achieve a following with collectors was the 1930 Model A coupé from Brooklin of Canada. An early Brooklin model from the 1970s, this coupé – as well as its Victoria sibling and the 2 door sedan version – are heavy, handbuilt white metal models. While these hefty models lack many of the details and body hardware parts found in today's models, they have glossy paint and are well crafted. They are also fairly abundant with each body style enjoying a production run of more than a thousand pieces. For a collector of 1930-31 Fords, these models are likely to be at the core of their collection.

There are few models of 1931-34 Ford vehicles except for a model truck kit from Berkshire Valley (USA), a thin supply of obsolete, toy-like replicas from Nostalgic Miniatures (USA), and the more detailed Auto Buff models.

Any Auto Buff model may be of special interest to a Ford model collector. Auto Buff (USA) was one of the first makers of handbuilt models and was a Ford specialist. It produced several models from the early 1930s and 1940s era. Made during the late 1970s and through to the early 1980s when model-making techniques were not as sophisticated as they are today, Auto Buff models are sometimes smaller-scaled than 1:43, but tend to have good proportions and quite a bit of detail. They're fairly rare.

Several companies – including Milestone Miniatures (UK) and Auto Buff – have produced replicas of the 1935-36 Ford. Mini Marque '43' (UK) made a number of 1936 Fords that vary widely in finish and detail. Later versions appear well finished and will not disappoint.

Flatbacks from 1937 are rare. Only Motor City USA released a little 2 door model as part of its less expensive USA models line. Approximately 500 of these exist. An extremely limited number of 1937 station wagons, modeled after film star Clark Gable's personal vehicle, were also released by Mini Marque '43'. No Ford handbuilt models from 1938 are known to exist.

There is a plethora of 1939 Ford trucks in sedan delivery, panel delivery and bus versions in several different liveries thanks to Durham Classics (Canada). Western Models (UK) and Motor City USA issued realistic, wood-bodied 1939 Ford station wagons. The latter was issued as late as 2003.

FORD

THE '40s

Although Auto Buff produced models of the 1940 Ford car in many different body styles, the finest replicas of that year's popular Standard and DeLuxe Ford are from Motor City USA, which offered a full assortment of body styles. In my opinion, they are under-priced with most selling at between $100 and $150.

Only Durham Classics offers a 1941 Ford. While not as detailed as its Motor City USA counterparts, these models are accurate in shape and size, sturdily constructed, and have clean castings with no burrs of metal or surface irregularities. If you care about authenticity, applying a little bare metal foil to these little white metal replicas brings them up to a very high standard of accuracy. There are no handbuilt 1942 Ford models.

Post-WWII, many makers chose to model 1946-48 Fords. All of the examples from this era are worth collecting. For affordability, you may want to find a resin Provence Moulage (France) or ECMA/Jedo 43 (France). Both are usually priced at under $100. Western's 1946 sedan is a good, mid-priced white metal model at $150. If money is no object, one of the few hundred woody Sportsman convertibles or wagons that Motor City USA issued are terrific finds at around $250-$300.

Light trucks from 1948-52 are available from US Model Mint (a Brooklin Models line), and Brooklin Models. Trucks from the 1953-55 period are available in several body variations and liveries from Durham Classics. Once again, it's possible to find an Auto Buff truck model for a song, at around $50.

The watershed year of 1949 saw only Kager (Germany) produce handbuilt resin convertibles, 4 door sedans, and station wagons in kit form and the odd built-up. Long out of production, these have clean castings, good proportions, and rarely change hands for more than $100.

1940 FORD DELUX 5 WINDOW COUPÉ AND 1940 FORD STANDARD 2 DOOR SEDAN BY MOTOR CITY USA. (AUTHOR COLLECTION)

THE '50s

1950 CUSTOM 4 DOOR SEDAN AND 1950 CUSTOM 2 DOOR SEDAN WITH FENDER SKIRTS FROM MOTOR CITY USA. (AUTHOR COLLECTION)

For the 1950-51 model year, Motor City USA issued all body styles produced by Ford. Some of the first models that the company built with full detailing, they typically trade in the $150-$300 price range, although I snapped one up at auction for less than $100.

Handbuilt 1952-54 Ford models are scarce, with a few resin and white metal examples from the defunct Oakland company (US) surfacing every so often on the aftermarket. For $50 or less it is possible to acquire one of the several thousand die-cast, hand-assembled models from the Argentinian company, Collectors' Classics. While not perfectly proportioned, these 1953 hardtop coupé and convertible models have nice brightwork, and come in a terrific assortment of authentic colors.

1955 and 1956 Ford models are plentiful in handbuilt form. Motor City USA's '55 Sunliner convertible, Crown Victoria, and Skyliner are superbly accurate, and Brooklin makes a nice affordable '56 2 door sedan at under $100. CCC (France) released a few hundred very delicate and extremely detailed resin and white metal convertible and Crown Victoria replicas.

For 1957, Mini Marque '43' issued a convertible and hardtop coupé of the top-of-the-line Fairlane. The company also produced a Ranchero pickup and Del Rio station wagon, all in white metal. The convertibles are quite common with up to 2000 produced and seldom cost more than $100. The hardtop, Ranchero and station wagon are less abundant with production of all three styles combined roughly equivalent to that of the convertible alone. For this reason, they tend to be more expensive and may still be available in hobby stores and stockists at close to their original $175-$225 retail price. In 2005, Brooklin issued a red 1957 Ranchero. At less than $100, this is a very nicely proportioned and finished handbuilt white metal model.

Ford in Miniature

Thunderbirds from 1955-57 are quite popular. Starting at the bottom of the price range (around $25) and progressing to the top (around $235) are examples from defunct Nostalgic Miniatures, Brooklin Models (including a gift set featuring a trio of Thunderbirds from 1955-57), Durham Classics, and finally, Conquest Models (Holland; now USA). Conquest issued a jewel-like T-Bird in 1993 that was available open or with top up. Less than 1000 of these models were made.

For model year 1958, Marque One Models (UK) produced Sunliner convertibles and Fairlane hardtop coupés in resin and white metal. Available in a few color combinations, these late 1980s models featured modern photo-etching technology that permitted finely detailed side mouldings, grillework and emblems. Western Models' fine, Custom 300 series four door sedans eclipsed the finishing of the Marque One models. Its 1:43 scale white metal version of the 1958 Ford family car is still being produced and is good value at around $150.

Edsel models spanning the entire production run of 1958-60 are plentiful with Brooklin leading the way. Its 1958 Citation open convertible and hardtop coupé can be bought at auction in the $50-75 price range. While the model's proportions are quite good, it is not very detailed. Mini Marque '43' also issued replicas of the same line and body style but with more detailing. These models were produced up until 2000 but can be acquired for between $75 and $150; a substantial discount from their $195 issue price. Earlier replicas from around 1990 are plainer than the later versions. Both of the British makers' models seem to ride low and have a curiously 'flat' appearance, more so than the real car.

Zaugg (Switzerland) released Pacer models in the late 1980s. While these models have very good proportions that surpass the replicas from Brooklin and Mini Marque '43', in my opinion they appear to be smaller than 1:45 scale and look somewhat out of place next to the other models mentioned here. Franklin Mint (USA) made a 1958 Citation convertible that is die-cast and toy-like next to the handbuilt models. Only one 1959 Edsel handbuilt model has been released. This is a very good two-toned Ranger sedan from Western.

The esthetically pleasing 1959 Ford was modeled by Western, which also issued open convertible, closed retractable, 4 door sedan, and Country Squire station wagon body styles. These replicas have finely detailed grilles that nicely mimic those of the original automobiles.

A few manufacturers issued Thunderbird models from 1958-60. Besides the more common 1959 Brooklin version and the very low production convertibles and hardtop coupés by artisan maker, Enchantment Land Coachbuilders (USA), only one other maker made replicas, although its original pattern was used by other companies: if you acquire a Jupiter/Belgium trucks (Belgium) or Mini Marque '43' 1958 or 1960 Thunderbird, you will enjoy a finely-detailed, well-proportioned and painstakingly finished handbuilt model that was originally produced by husband and wife team Alistair and Sally Duncan of A&S Models (UK) during the late 1980s to early 1990s.

The '60s

If you want a 1960 handbuilt Edsel model, only Brooklin has seen fit to make one, in an open convertible version. A late 1990s release, it's a good example of Brooklin's accurate patterns and high build quality.

Handbuilt models of 1960 full-sized Ford automobiles are limited to an open Sunliner by Brooklin that is moderately detailed and well-priced at below $100.

Milestone Miniatures (South Africa) made the first replica of the fledgling 1960 Falcon. This is a very scarce model. Other Falcon models were issued representing the 1963 model year. Brooklin made a few thousand light green Futura hardtops and, in 2005, released a more detailed and reasonably priced, red convertible. Trax (Australia) has issued several body styles and die-cast versions of the 1960-62 Australian Falcon that are very close to the American styling aside from the placement of the steering wheel. These are plentiful and at $20-$40 are bargains.

Examples of handbuilt full and mid-sized Ford models from

1958 THUNDERBIRD 4 PASSENGER 2 DOOR HARD TOP FROM A&S MODELMAKERS, AND 1957 THUNDERBIRD 2 PASSENGER CONVERTIBLE WITH REMOVABLE PORTHOLE TOP FROM CONQUEST MODELS. (AUTHOR COLLECTION)

1960 FORD SUNLINER TOP UP CONVERTIBLE, IN WHITE METAL BY BROOKLIN MODELS. (AUTHOR COLLECTION)

FORD

the 1960s are few and far between. SMTS (UK) modeled the 1963 Ford Galaxie 2 door hardtop coupé, convertible, and Country Squire station wagon for Fa. Daimler House (Holland) in 1990-91. These are rarely available today although I recently found a new Country Squire from a French stockist at around $300. SMTS still produces a stock car race version of the hardtop. For the 1968 model year, Milestone Miniatures offers a Torino convertible and fastback that is also available from K&D Automobile (USA).

Mustangs have been quite popular with builders of handbuilt models. In addition to the simple Nostalgic Miniatures, is the fine Precision Miniatures (USA) 1965 open convertible, notchback coupé, and fastback coupé which are nicely finished and detailed models produced in the 1980s. Brooklin's 1965 convertible and 1968 fastback are fairly abundant and pleasing, as is Western Models' more detailed 1965 Mustang open convertible. Less common are versions by French builder, Century, Heco, and Starter, Illustra (UK), and Ma Scale Models (USA). These latter models have been discontinued but appear sporadically in garage sales and on-line auctions such as Vectis and eBay.

Finally, Thunderbird replicas for 1961-63, 1965, and 1967 are available. Zaugg and Tin Wizard made nice hardtop, convertible, roadster, and pace car versions of the early '60s T-Bird. Tin Wizard sells these on its website. Brooklin built a nicely proportioned 1965 convertible, and a very accurate and nicely detailed 1967 hardtop that captures the cleanliness and simplicity of line of the original automobile.

TOP: 1930 FORD MODEL A VICTORIA SEDAN BY BROOKLIN, NUMBER BRK-3X. THIS ORANGE VERSION WAS ISSUED FOR WEBER'S 72ND ANNIVERSARY IN 1989 AND IS 1 OF 72. IT IS HIGHLY COLLECTIBLE AND WOULD SELL FOR AROUND $300 TODAY. (COURTESY D MATHYSSEN)

Model-by-model 1930-1938

The 1930 to 1938 period saw a number of dramatic changes in North American motorcars as the automobile came of age. Manufacturing techniques improved steadily and materials changed. The use of wood as a structural component disappeared in all but station wagons. By the middle of the decade stylists had real power that dramatically changed the way cars looked. The '2 box' (engine house and passenger compartment) configuration of cars was replaced by a '3 box' model, with trunks becoming an integral component of automobile bodies.

At the Ford Motor Company the speed of change was reflected in the relatively early disappearance of the square-shaped Model A, and arrival of the very popular V-8 Ford with its more rakish appearance that included slanted

MIDDLE: BROOKLIN ALSO MADE THE 1930 FORD MODEL A COUPÉ, NUMBER BRK-5. ISSUED JUST AFTER BRK-3, THIS MODEL HAD THE SAME OLDER VERSION ANGEL/HALL WHEELS AND TIRES (NAMED AFTER ITS CREATOR) AS THE BRK-3. IT, TOO, IS RARE AS THIS EARLIEST BLACK CANADIAN VERSION. (COURTESY D MATHYSSEN)

BOTTOM: 1930 FORD MODEL A COUPÉ BY BROOKLIN, NUMBER BRK-5. 300 OF THESE LITTLE COUPÉ MODELS WERE PRODUCED AS SOUVENIRS FOR THE PHILADELPHIA FIRE DEPARTMENT. (COURTESY D MATHYSSEN)

LEFT: 1930 FORD MODEL A VICTORIA SEDAN BY BROOKLIN (NUMBER BRK-3X). BROOKLIN MODELS ISSUED A SCALE REPLICA OF THIS IMMENSELY POPULAR MOTORCAR IN 1976 WHEN THE BUILDER WAS BASED IN CANADA. EARLIEST MODELS HAD NO WINDOW TRANSPARENCIES (GLASS). ISSUED IN SEVERAL COLOR VARIATIONS, IT WAS DISCONTINUED IN 1985 AFTER NO MORE THAN A FEW THOUSAND MODELS WERE PRODUCED. (COURTESY D MATHYSSEN)

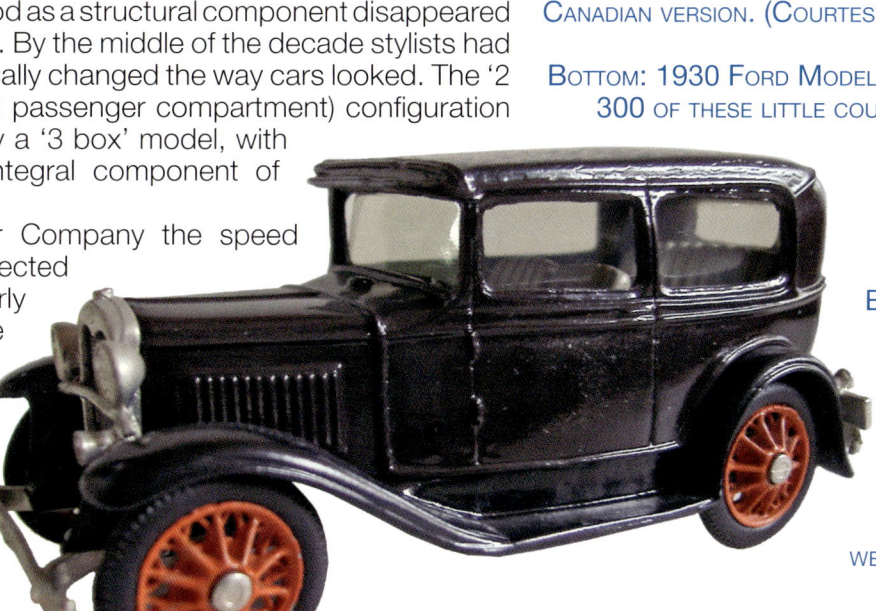

Ford in miniature

radiator grilles, rounder, fuller fender treatment, and sleeker contours at the leading faces of body components. Ford was sometimes late in adopting certain mechanical innovations such as hydraulic brakes, but Ford styling during this period kept pace with other builders: the 1937 model, with its recessed, fender-mounted, triangular-shaped headlights and 'flatback' styling, is proof of this. Handbuilt model-making of motorcars from the 1930-1938 period has been largely confined to 1930 and 1935-36.

CONTINUED PAGE 22

1931 Model AA light van by Enchantment Land Coachbuilders. Other companies, such as Berkshire Valley, offer realistic-looking late 1920s and early 1930s Ford trucks. However, they are in 'O' gauge (1:48 scale) for model railroad layouts. This model is one of a kind, handmade in resin by Jerry Rettig of Enchantment Land Coachbuilders. (Courtesy J Rettig)

1934 Ford coupé with rumble seat in black, and 1934 Ford top up roadster in beige and brown by Auto Buff, model numbers 19 and 21. These early handbuilt white metal Fords were issued in the late 1970s and early 1980s. (Courtesy J Rettig)

1928 Model A coupé. 500 of these tan and black numbers were produced in 2005 by Minichamps. A die-cast model that uses mass production techniques, it retails at around $40, making it an affordable, accurately proportioned and highly detailed model that will fit in with higher-end handbuilt models in the collector's display cabinet. This passenger side view of the 1928 Model A by Minichamps shows the maker's careful paintwork and details such as the running board mounted toolbox. While a significant advancement on the Tin Lizzie, particularly in its protective closed-car mode, the model still displayed elements of its horseless carriage origin, as shown by its boxy shape and narrow wheels. This would change in less than half a decade with the debut of the V-8 Fords. Minichamps model number 8101. (Author collection)

1932 Model A station wagon in Buttercup Yellow. Released by Enchantment Land Coachbuilders in very small numbers, this is a resin model with hand-painted woodgrain. (Courtesy J Rettig)

1931 Ford Model A open roadster in pewter from Danbury Mint. This cheerful yellow and orange model is scarce today. (Courtesy J Rettig)

1932 Ford 3-window coupé hot rod. In its final days of production during 2004, Durham Classics issued a line of handbuilt white metal hot rods, some with engines exposed. This is model CC01. Only 1000 of these, in a variety of colors, were produced. The street version of this 1932 model was never issued. (Durham Classics Automotive Miniatures)

1933 Ford V-8 cabriolet. A die-cast model released in 2004 for the Australian market (note the location of the steering wheel for right hand drive). Made by Minichamps. (Courtesy J Rettig)

Rear views of the 1935 Fordor touring sedan and sedan delivery. Note the externally mounted spare wheel cover on the sedan that revealed the red wheel rims. By 1937 the spare wheel was hidden in the trunk. As was common in replicas made during the 1970s and 1980s, rear lights are red painted enamel. Gradually, this practice was replaced by the use of red foil that, though more fragile, is more convincing in appearance. Rextoys model numbers 45 and 42. (Author collection)

A pair of Rextoys models from the author's collection. A 1935 Ford sedan delivery finished as a Ford dealership parts delivery vehicle (number 45), and a 1935 Ford Fordor touring sedan (number 42). To amortize the high production costs of producing dies, Rextoys models were offered in several body styles, colors, and liveries. Originally retailing at in excess of $30, these models have tended to retain their value even though they are frequently available at auction, due, no doubt, to their construction of durable materials, high assembly standards, and unique choice of subject that was limited to the 1935 Ford, 1938 Cadillac and rare 1940 Packard. With the exception of a small number of ELC and Mini Marque '43' 1935 Ford models, builders have shied away from this model year, perhaps because of the abundance of available Rextoys. Notice how the radiator cap is molded as part of the larger radiator shell and grille. If this were a handbuilt model it is likely that these three parts would be separate. Moreover, as builders sought greater realism, by the 1990s the grille was 'blackwashed' with paint or even photo-etched so that the spaces behind the grille would be in shadow, as they would appear on the actual vehicle. Still, this is a great effort for a low-priced replica. (Author collection)

In 1935 a single wiper blade was used to clear the windshield in front of the driver's face. The historically accurate Ford signage on this 1935 sedan delivery gives it authenticity. Rextoys model number 45. (Author collection)

1935 Ford sedan delivery in Texaco livery, Rextoys model number 45. (Courtesy Toys for Collectors USA)

The 1935 Ford Fordor touring sedan was a lot of car that competed well with rivals Chevrolet and Plymouth. With a reliable, modern V-8 and elements of streamlining such as the canted radiator shell, this beauty also sported red wheels and canvas sunroof. Rextoys model number 42. (Author collection)

1935 Siebert limousine hearse. This striking Charcoal Grey model was handmade in resin by Jerry Rettig of Enchantment Land Coachbuilders; model number F3. (Courtesy J Rettig)

1935 Ford coupé. Die-cast by Team Calibre, this highly detailed model has many movable parts. Originally made as a race car, this model has been converted to street form by Jerry Rettig. (Courtesy J Rettig)

Nostalgic Miniatures, an early Ford model specialist, made this attractive yellow white metal 1936 Ford roadster, number 234. This photograph illustrates just how much streamlining had influenced Ford design by 1936. With no straight lines in sight, this French Curved design included a fully enclosed trunk that may have held a rumble seat. (Courtesy J Rettig)

1936 Ford top up phaeton in a metallic wine color. Handmade in pewter by Collector Case, it was also available from the builder with the top down and as a 3 window coupé and roadster. This example, model number 608, has received extra detailing. (Courtesy J Rettig)

Several makers have modeled 1936 Ford models. Forty Third Avenue (from Milestone Miniatures) is responsible for this 3-window coupé, model number AA5. Forty Third Avenue also modeled an open rumble seat roadster, number AA12. These fairly simple models with patterns dating to the 1980s are now out of production. (Courtesy J Rettig)

1936 Ford cabriolet, top down, navy with grey interior and exposed rumble seat by CCC Models of France. Nicely detailed, factory-built resin model that was made in the early 1990s and has long been out of production. Mounted on removable Plexiglas base. CCC model number 2. (Courtesy J Rettig) Inset: One of the features that often distinguishes handbuilt models from their more plentiful die-cast counterparts is the handbuilt's more extensive interior detail. The instrument panel on this model has black dial faces with white markings, knobs picked out in ivory, and even a glove box door handle. An especially nice touch is the long-handled gearshift and the horn button mounted in the centre of the authentic-looking steering wheel. Sometimes with 1:43 scale models the steering wheel seems too thick but that's not the case with this accurately rendered model. (Courtesy J Hartman)

Mini Marque '43' 1936 sedan delivery, number 6, with 'Ford' signage and colors. A popular way to offer variety and stimulate sales is to issue special liveries for the public as well as those commissioned for companies and events. An example of this is this Ford and a '36 Packard sedan delivery that Mini Marque '43' issued in Coca-Cola livery. (Courtesy D Larsen)

FORD

1936 SEDAN DELIVERY, NUMBER 6, BY MINI MARQUE '43' IN INDIAN HILL DAIRY LIVERY. (AUTHOR COLLECTION)

1935 AND 1936 SEDAN DELIVERY MODELS SIDE-BY-SIDE ILLUSTRATE MINOR ANNUAL STYLING CHANGES, PRIMARILY IN THE GRILLE AREA. THE PRACTICE OF MAKING CHANGES FOR STYLING'S SAKE REACHED A CLIMAX IN THE 1960S WHEN 'PLANNED OBSOLESCENCE' WAS INTRODUCED TO THE AUTOMOBILE MANUFACTURERS' LEXICON. AT ABOUT ONE-FIFTH THE VALUE OF THE YELLOW, HANDMADE WHITE METAL MINI MARQUE '43' MODEL ON THE RIGHT, THE BLUE DIE-CAST REXTOYS SEDAN DELIVERY ACQUITS ITSELF WELL, ALTHOUGH THERE ARE THOUSANDS AVAILABLE ON THE AFTERMARKET COMPARED WITH JUST A HUNDRED OF THE HANDBUILT MODEL. REXTOYS MODEL NUMBER 45 AND MINI MARQUE '43' MODEL NUMBER 8. (AUTHOR COLLECTION)

THIS MINI MARQUE '43' EXAMPLE IS THE NICEST FINISHED AND DETAILED 1:43 SCALE MODEL OF THE 1935 FORD PHAETON PACE CAR MADE. IT WAS ALSO AVAILABLE AS A STREET VERSION TOP UP IN GLOSSY RED, 100 EXAMPLES OF WHICH WERE MADE. THESE REPLICAS COMPRISE MORE THAN 75 PIECES, AND EXTENSIVE DETAILING INCLUDES SEPARATE DOOR HANDLES AND WINDOW WINDERS CRAFTED FROM PLATED WHITE METAL. MODEL NUMBER MMQ-45. (AUTHOR COLLECTION)

MINI MARQUE '43' MADE SEVERAL VERSIONS OF THE 1935 AND 1936 FORD. IN ADDITION TO THIS FINE PHAETON AND SEDAN DELIVERY, A FEW HUNDRED ROADSTERS (NUMBER MMQ-6) WERE CRAFTED. MODEL NUMBERS MMQ-45A AND MMQ-8. (AUTHOR COLLECTION)

SOME 1937 FLATBACK 2 DOOR SEDANS WERE EQUIPPED WITH A WEAK 60HP V-8 ENGINE. THIS WELL-DETAILED MODEL IS A WHITE METAL, HANDBUILT USA MODELS OFFERING, NUMBER 37, WHICH WAS PRODUCED IN SMALL NUMBERS IN BLACK, GREY, AND TAN. (AUTHOR COLLECTION)

1936 FORD LONG WHEELBASE SEDAN IN A GLOSSY NAVY BLUE FROM ASHTON MODELS. THIS BUILDER – NOW BASED IN POLAND – IS KNOWN FOR ITS SPECTACULAR, COMPREHENSIVE LINE OF HISTORIC FIRE SERVICE REPLICAS SUCH AS FIRE ENGINES, PUMPERS AND LADDER TRUCKS. NOT SURPRISINGLY, THIS MODEL, NUMBER 1, WAS ALSO PRODUCED AS A MORE COMMON BATTALION FIRE CHIEF VERSION, NUMBERED 10A. (AUTHOR COLLECTION)

1937 FORD FLATBACK 2 DOOR SEDAN IN BROWN; 1939 FORD STATION WAGON IN FOLKESTONE GRAY, AND 1940 DELUXE CONVERTIBLE IN MAROON. ALL THREE MODELS ARE BY MOTOR CITY USA. (AUTHOR COLLECTION)

Ford in miniature

Model-by-model — 1939-1948

1939 STATION WAGON IN WHITE METAL FROM MOTOR CITY USA. THE FIRST MODEL IN THE AMERICAN MODELS LINE FROM A PATTERN BY THE ILLUSTRIOUS PETER KENNA OF ENGLAND. MODEL NUMBER AM-1. (AUTHOR COLLECTION)

Quite a few handbuilt models are available for 1939-48 although no 1942 models were issued.

One of the cleanest model lines to come out of Detroit in 1940 was Ford's. Over half a million Standard and DeLuxe models were made for the model year, good for second place behind Chevrolet in model production. These cars were reliable as well and, today, many collectors take pride in owning one. The models illustrated here were produced in the early 1990s by Motor City USA. Part of this builder's lesser-detailed USA line, they boast glossy paint and flawless proportions.

CONTINUED PAGE 33

The period 1939 to 1948 covers a fascinating time for mankind that saw amazing technological advances: television and robotics showcased at the 1939 New York World's Fair, and the conflagration of a second global war. On the North American automotive scene, 1941 is often regarded as the culmination of the "streamlining influence" when virtually every automaker offered an attractive and mechanically reliable product.

This was a productive yet tumultuous time at Ford that witnessed the passing of scion, Henry Ford and his son, Edsel. It was a period that saw the highs of the beautiful new 1939 Ford and Mercury automobiles speeding around their closed ramp at the World's Fair, and the lows of the post-war years when the company struggled with old ideas and a leadership vacuum until Henry Ford II began to right the ship.

In 1939 Ford replaced its pleasant 1938 'flatbacks' with 'fastbacks' which possessed a cleanliness of line that makes them a very collectible car today. These 1939 and 1940 automobiles evolved into the middle of the road 1946-48 models that people were happy to have during the sellers' market of that period.

1939 FORD BUS FROM DURHAM CLASSICS. NUMBER DC-23A. DURHAM CLASSICS ISSUED NUMEROUS VARIATIONS OF THIS MODEL. (COURTESY D LARSEN)

1939 ¾ TON PANEL DELIVERY. A SUBSTANTIAL HANDBUILT WHITE METAL MODEL IN THE LIVERY OF THE CHICAGO HERALD, COMPLETE WITH CALL-OUT BOARD ON THE SIDE. FROM DURHAM CLASSICS, MODEL NUMBER DC-3. (AUTHOR COLLECTION)

ABOVE LEFT: A LONG OBSOLETE 1939 STATION WAGON FROM BRITAIN'S WESTERN MODELS. DARK GREEN WITH SIMULATED ASH PANELS AND OAK FRAMES, THIS IS A LIMITED EDITION AND WAS APPARENTLY NEVER ASSIGNED A MODEL NUMBER. SCARCE. (COURTESY D LARSEN)

LEFT: ONE OF THE EARLIEST VERSIONS OF THE 1939 FORD SATION WAGON WAS THIS NOSTALGIC MINIATURES MODEL, NUMBER 279. PRODUCED IN WHITE METAL AT A REPUTED 1:42 SCALE, THE FINISH IS SOMEWHAT CRUDE BY TODAY'S STANDARDS, ALTHOUGH THE BUILDER CAPTURED ITS STYLING AND PROPORTIONS WELL. (COURTESY J RETTIG)

1939 FORD RAIL BUS. FINISHED IN BRIGHT YELLOW WITH UNION PACIFIC LOGOS ON DOORS, RAIL WHEELS AND 'O' GAUGE TRACK FOR DISPLAY. 250 PIECES WERE RELEASED, DURHAM CLASSICS NUMBER DC-17A. (COURTESY DURHAM CLASSICS AUTOMOTIVE MINIATURES)

FORD

1940 SEDAN DELIVERY. 150 PIECES WERE ISSUED IN 1985 FOR THE MAIDENHEAD STATIC MODEL COLLECTORS' CLUB. BROOKLIN MODEL NUMBER BRK-9. (COURTESY D MATHYSSEN)

ABOVE: 1940 SEDAN DELIVERY FROM BROOKLIN, MODEL NUMBER BRK-9. A POPULAR MODEL BY HANDMADE STANDARDS, THE BRITISH MODEL BUILDER PRODUCED MORE THAN 5000 OF THESE IN A VARIETY OF LIVERIES BETWEEN 1979 AND 1993. THIS IS THE STANDARD MODEL WITH FORD LOGOS AND SIGN, 'O'NEILL LTD SALES, PARTS, SERVICE' THAT WAS DISCONTINUED IN 1991. (COURTESY D MATHYSSEN)

LEFT: 1940 SEDAN DELIVERY. AFTER BROOKLIN MODELS MOVED FROM CANADA TO BATH, ENGLAND, THE COMPANY CREATED 800 MODELS IN THE LIVERY OF HUGGET ELECTRICAL, A COMPANY FROM BATH. MODEL NUMBER BRK-9. (COURTESY D MATHYSSEN)

THE SALVATION ARMY HOPE CENTRE LIVERY WAS THE SUBJECT OF THIS 1940 SEDAN DELIVERY REPLICA FROM BROOKLIN MODELS, NUMBER BRK-9. (COURTESY D MATHYSSEN)

FOR ITS 60TH ANNIVERSARY, GERMAN STORE, SPIELWAREN DANHAUSEN, HAD BROOKLIN MODELS PRODUCE 1940 FORD SEDAN DELIVERY MODELS IN FOUR DIFFERENT COLOR COMBINATIONS. THIS IS THE FIRST ISSUE THAT DISPLAYS THE STORE'S NAME IN AN EARLY STYLE OF SCRIPT. (COURTESY D MATHYSSEN)

A CHEERFUL YELLOW WAS USED BY BROOKLIN MODELS FOR THE 16TH JAMES LEAKE AUCTION OF 1988 FORD SEDAN DELIVERY, MODEL NUMBER BRK-9. (COURTESY D MATHYSSEN)

1940 FORD SEDAN DELIVERY FROM BROOKLIN MODELS. THIS IS THE RIGHT HAND DRIVE 'WEETIES' VERSION MADE FOR THE AUSTRALIAN MARKET IN 1990. MODEL NUMBER BRK-9. (COURTESY D MATHYSSEN)

FIFTY BURGUNDY JUNK MODELS WERE ISSUED BY BROOKLIN FOR JIM, ULLI, AND NICKY KING OF HOLLAND. MODEL NUMBER BRK-9. (COURTESY D MATHYSSEN)

Ford in miniature

A popular item to celebrate toy shows, this time in Toledo, Ohio in 1979. 128 of these 1940 Ford sedan delivery models were created by Brooklin. Model number BRK-9. (Courtesy D Mathyssen)

Above: 1940 models were very popular with enthusiasts and builders. This is an early example of the 5-window coupé, handmade in white metal by HeiTech of Australia. Model number 1, it measures out at about 1:44 scale. (Courtesy J Rettig)

One of Brooklin's most popular models, the 1940 sedan delivery was often used as a souvenir for companies, events, and charities such as the 200 models issued for the National Deaf Children's Society. (Courtesy D Mathyssen)

1940 Ford Siebert limousine-style hearse. Handcrafted in resin by Enchantment Land Coachbuilders, only 25 of these models were released. (Courtesy J Rettig)

A well-detailed and nicely-proportioned die-cast model of the 1940 Ford coupé from Team Caliber. (Courtesy J Rettig)

1940 Ford Deluxe 2 door coupé number 8 in black, and 1940 convertible number 9 from Auto Buff. Issued by the now defunct California builder in 1981 and handbuilt from white metal. These models are said to be closer to 1:48 scale. (Courtesy J Rettig)

FORD

1940 Ford Deluxe open convertible, 1940 Ford Standard 2 door sedan, 1940 Ford Standard 4 door sedan, 1940 Ford pickup. Models from Motor City USA. (Author collection)

1940 Deluxe open convertible. This Design Studios model, number 9D ('D' for top down) has superb finishing, proportions, and accurate details down to the photo-etched script and emblems. Note the wiper placement and headlight lenses. (Author collection)

Three 1940 Ford models from Motor City USA which represent the different trim levels of the original vehicle and the model company. At left is an early USA Models 1940 Standard 4 door sedan in Garnet Maroon (number 8). An example of the company's entry level USA line, issued in the early 1990s, it has few details; even the wipers are body-colored and part of the main casting. The jet black number in the middle from the mid-1990s is a USA line 1940 Ford Standard 2 door sedan, number 11. This has chrome moldings and the wipers are picked out in silver paint. On the right is a mid-1990s Design Studios 1940 Ford Deluxe 5-window coupé in Mandarin Maroon. It has extensive chrome detailing, resin headlight lenses, photo-etched script, and an interior with many separate parts. Model number DS-9D. (Author collection)

1940 Ford Deluxe convertible in profile. Even the hubcaps have 'Ford' stamped in red enamel. Design Studios model number DS-9D from Motor City USA of California. (Author collection)

1940 pickup in dark green. USA Models number 14 in white metal. (Author collection)

This rear three-quarter view of the 1940 Ford convertible by Design Studio shows the flawless proportions and great detailing of this model, right down to the high mounted center brake light, chrome gas filler cap, and twist-style trunk latch. (Author collection)

1940 Standard 4 door sedan. USA-8, in maroon. Part of the builder's less detailed USA line, it boasts glossy paint, solid assembly and excellent proportions. (Author collection)

No fewer than four shades of maroon were offered by the Ford Motor Company in 1940. This is a pleasantly detailed, 5-window coupé ('opera coupé' would be too grand a name for a Ford body style) in Mandarin Maroon from Motor City USA's Design Studios line. Model number DS-9C. (Author collection)

Pair of 2 door models. The 1940 Deluxe coupé on the left in Madarin Maroon is a well-detailed Design Studios offering, number DS-9C, and the black 1940 Standard 2 door sedan number USA-11. Both handmade, white metal models were issued by Motor City USA in the mid-1990s. (Author collection)

1940 Standard 2 door sedan. This is from Motor City USA's USA Model line, number 11. Although very well finished, it has fewer details than the Design Studio convertible models pictured previously. (Author collection)

1941 Ford 2 door sedans in Sheffield Grey and Lockhaven Green. A pair of well-detailed and technically accurate die-cast models produced in China for Fleer Collectibles. The model on the left has a common feature of lower cost die-cast models: the headlights have a pronounced black spot in the centre resembling the pupil of an eye. The lens is essentially an inexpensive clear plastic peg that is inserted in a hole in the fender. The hole is in shadow and appears as a black spot when seen from the outside. Handbuilt models do not have this dark spot because they often use different types of headlight that have a reflective lens, are made of white metal, or are attached directly to the fender itself and not through a hole. The headlights of the green model on the right have been modified by the author who has used bare metal foil to cover the lens. (Author collection)

FORD

A pair of 1941 Ford 2 door sedan models; 1:43 scale die-casts from Fleer Collectibles. Note the painted chrome trim and tail lights. This is a lot of model for $15 which, with a few simple touches at the hands of a model-maker, can offer a high level of realism. (Author collection)

1948 top down convertible by Auto Buff, number 5. A nicely detailed model which has accurate proportions and nice details such as fender skirts. (Courtesy J Rettig)

Above: An interesting subject for a replica, a 1942 Ford pickup from Gearbox. A die-cast model that in 2006 would sell in the $10-15 range, it has amazing detail, including opening doors and liftgate, and front wheels that can be positioned as though the model is turning. The only flaw, and it is amusing, are 'hinges' for the cab door. When the doors are opened, the hinges move out with the door, showing that they are part of the door itself.
(Author collection)

1947 Ford Sportsman convertible in red with hand-detailed woodgrain. French builder CCC issued model number 1 as both kit and factory-built models. This is a kit built by a modeler. (Courtesy J Rettig)

1941 club coupé. The only handbuilt 1941 Fords are from Durham Classics. 200 were issued in Folkestone Grey. Originally a fairly plain model, this version has received quite a bit of detailing with bare metal chrome foil. A convertible version, number DC-20, was also offered in top up and open body styles. Model number 15. (Courtesy D Larsen)

27

Ford in miniature

1948 Deluxe 2 door club coupé. AMT, the well-known kit and promotional model-maker produced a 1:43 scale kit during the early 1990s. This model was painted, assembled and detailed by highly regarded modeller, Bruce Arnold, who also created the patterns and models for Cadillac Motor Division. (Courtesy D Larsen)

Western's number 77 1946 Fordor in taxicab garb with authentic signs and other details. (Courtesy Western Models Ltd)

1946 sedan and station wagon from Provence Moulage of France, numbers 179 and 120 in resin with white metal parts. Both of these models tend to be quite scarce today. (Courtesy J Rettig)

1946 4 door sedan from Western Models. These model number 77s are handmade from white metal and have a very good level of detail. (Courtesy Western Models Ltd)

1948 sedan delivery in light blue. Equipe Tron handcrafted this extremely rare, well-detailed resin model. (Courtesy J Rettig)

Using the authentic colors and emblems of the Missouri State Police, Western Models' 1946 Ford, number 77P, evokes a time when Ford vehicles – with their strong flathead V-8 mills – were the preference of many North American law enforcement agencies. (Courtesy Western Models Ltd)

Produced in 2005, this IXO die-cast model of the 1947 Ford 4 door shows what a good quality mass-production model can look like. Retail price is around $30. (Courtesy J Rettig)

1948 Ford station wagon. Not a handbuilt model but an inexpensive die-cast replica produced in China by Yatming, which retails for around ten dollars. (Courtesy J Rettig)

1948 F1 pickup. The iconic little red truck was selected by Ford, in concert with the manufacturer Minichamps, to be one of thirteen models sold in the 'Heart and Soul' set to commemorate Ford Motor Company's 100th anniversary. (Author collection)

1948 F1 pickup, issued by Brooklin Models in 2005, model number CSV-01 is in the livery of the Grottoes, Virginia Volunteer Fire Department. (Courtesy D Mathyssen)

1948 F1 pickup as a light fire truck from Ford's Richmond, California plant. Brooklin Models. (Courtesy D Mathyssen)

FORD

Brooklin's excellent 1947 station wagon number BRK-83. This is a superbly rendered handbuilt model that has won accolades in scale model magazines. A very good model in its price range. (Courtesy D Mathyssen)

1947 station wagon as issued in yellow as a limited edition souvenir of the October 2000 Modelex Show. Number BRK-83. (Courtesy D Mathyssen)

Ford in miniature

1947 and 1950 Ford station wagons from Motor City USA in Parrot Green and Cambridge Maroon. Handmade in white metal with terrific wood grain. Despite the shared bloodline of these two models, they are substantially different. The 1947 model is the last Ford station wagon to have wood as an integral part of its structure. In 1949 the steel-bodied (with wood inlay) Custom Deluxe station wagon, later to be named 'Country Squire', was introduced and became the favorite wagon of North American families. (Author collection)

Above: Is that a real car? Motor City USA's spectacular 1947 station wagon, number MC-72. This handbuilt, white metal replica has phenomenal proportions, assembly quality, finishing, and detail. The price? Around $275. (Author collection)

The station wagon was part of Ford's Super Deluxe series in 1947, the top trim level. At a base price of $1972, it cost half as much again as the lowest priced 2 door coupé. Yet it was not the costliest Ford that year. This distinction went to the wood-bodied Sportsman convertible which was $310 more than the wagon. (Author collection)

1947 Super Deluxe station wagon. Last of Ford's wood-bodied station wagons, built using a traditional construction process going back more than 100 years. Noted for its devotion to realism, Motor City USA ensures that details – such as the tiny wood fasteners used in the early wood-bodied cars – are depicted. This 1:43 scale model, unlike cheaper die-cast models, but like the original 1:1 motorcar, is comprised of several separate structural pieces. Motor City USA number 72. (Author collection)

Ford

Model-by-model — 1949-1951

1949 was a crucial year in Ford Motor Company's history, as the company sought to recapture market share lost to more interesting and diverse products from most of the other American automobile manufacturers. Ford's return to a vibrant, competitive manufacturer was due in large measure to the simple, slab-sided

1950 Custom club coupé; 1950 Custom 2 door sedan, and 1950 Custom 4 door sedan from Motor City USA. (Author collection)

This quite nicely done resin 2 door sedan is an Oakland model number 1. Auto Buff and Zaugg also made 1950 models in white metal, although they are so scarce I could not find photographs of them. The castings for this Oakland originated with Auto Buff. All three builders issued these models in tiny quantities and, as a result, they are quite rare today. This Oakland model will command $50-$150 on the aftermarket. (Courtesy J Rettig)

Swiss builder Jurg Zaugg produced this, now scarce, 1950 Club coupé in resin during the early 1980s. It has quite good detailing and finishing for its day. Zaugg model number 120. (Courtesy J Rettig)

1949 Ford. Its light, sleek styling appealed to a war-weary public, and symbolized the new Ford Motor Company run by Henry Ford II and his 'Whiz Kids'.

Elite scale model car maker, Motor City USA, chose the mildly reworked and improved 1950-1951 Ford as the basis for one of its earlier runs of handbuilt models. The handbuilt models from this American west coast company are noted for their extreme accuracy, loving details, and careful assembly. I have spoken to quite a few collectors of handbuilts from various builders who handle their models delicately but lose parts frequently. I have yet to meet a person who has had the same problem with a Motor City USA model.

CONTINUED PAGE 42

1949 business coupé by White Rose Collectibles. A die-cast model made in the tens of thousands, it is available for around $10 and, for the money, is an accurately proportioned and adequately detailed model. Ertl also made a nice model that is not as common and has been used as the basis for the ELC and Kager models, and Provence Moulage resin-bodied transkits. (Courtesy J Rettig)

Ford in miniature

Die-cast 1949 Ford Woody wagon from Franklin Mint from its Cars of The Fifties collection. Modifications by Bruce Arnold include chrome foil, new tires, stained wood framing and panel inserts. Says Bruce: "When Franklin Mint introduced the 1:43 world to fully detailed die-cast American cars, no-one knew what to expect. The early advertising stills of the Cars of the Fifties series showed repainted Mini Marque '43' and Western models mixed with some original prototypes. The production pieces were not Franklin Mint's crown jewels and came under some criticism. But they didn't give up. There were actually running changes that constantly improved new editions until they were discontinued. Their next two series, Cars of the 60s and Classic Cars, were the last 1:43 models made by Franklin Mint." Bruce Arnold assisted FM with development of the much-improved 60s collection. (Courtesy B Arnold)

Another fine 1949 Ford, issued as a kit by Germany's Kager and built up by Greg Gunn of Ohio. This is a well-proportioned model that captures the simplicity and lightness of the 1949 lines. How exciting it must have been when Dearborn's sleek new products were introduced after the warmed-over pre-war offerings from what was then the number 3 automaker! (Author collection)

Most station wagons had hidden spare wheels by the early 1950s. Rather than enclosing them inside the passenger compartment, the 1949 Ford hid its wheel within a body-colored cover attached to the tailgate. This practice would re-emerge with smaller 'SUVs' during the 1990s. (Author collection)

1949 and 1950 Country Squire station wagons from two different builders. The beige, resin-bodied beauty by Kager has slightly fewer details and relies on the modeler to add details such as hand-painted wood fasteners. The white metal maroon Motor City USA model, number 13, has extensive details molded into the metal and 'wood' cladding. The Kager is a one-piece cast body whereas the Motor City USA model has five main structural pieces. Both are fabulous. (Author collection)

FORD

THE 1950 FORD ACQUIRED FURTHER ADORNMENT IN ITS SECOND YEAR TO APPEAR SOMEWHAT MORE SUBSTANTIAL. THESE SCALE MODELS ACTUALLY VARY GREATLY IN WEIGHT DUE TO THE MATERIALS USED. THE BEIGE RESIN MODEL WEIGHS ABOUT 4 OUNCES/113 GRAMS AND THE MAROON WHITE METAL MODEL TIPS THE SCALES AT AROUND 12 OUNCES/340 GRAMS. (AUTHOR COLLECTION)

1950 FORD COUNTRY SQUIRE 2 DOOR STATION WAGON BY MOTOR CITY USA. AN EXTRAORDINARILY DETAILED REPLICA THAT BOASTS MORE THAN 80 PARTS AND AN AUTHENTIC CAMBRIDGE MAROON AUTOMOTIVE PAINT JOB. MODEL NUMBER MC-13. (AUTHOR COLLECTION)

TOP ROW FROM LEFT TO RIGHT: 1951 VICTORIA HARD TOP COUPÉ; 1951 CUSTOM CONVERTIBLE; 1950 DELUXE SQUAD CAR; 1950 CUSTOM 4 DOOR SEDAN; 1950 CUSTOM CONVERTIBLE. FRONT ROW FROM LEFT: 1950 COUNTRY SQUIRE STATION WAGON; 1950 CUSTOM BUSINESS COUPÉ; 1950 CUSTOM 2 DOOR SEDAN WITH FENDER SKIRTS; 1950 CRESTLINER 2 DOOR SEDAN WITH VINYL ROOF. ALL MODELS ARE FROM MOTOR CITY USA. (AUTHOR COLLECTION)

OVERALL, FORD PRODUCED 130,000 CLUB COUPÉ MODELS IN 1950 IN BOTH DELUXE AND CUSTOM DELUXE TRIM LEVELS. THIS IS A LARGE NUMBER BUT VERY MUCH FEWER THAN THE MOST POPULAR BODY STYLE, WHICH WAS THE 2 DOOR SEDAN. FEWER THAN 1000 OF THIS MOTOR CITY USA MODEL, NUMBER MC-11, WERE ISSUED. (AUTHOR COLLECTION)

1950 CUSTOM CLUB COUPÉ BY MOTOR CITY USA OF CALIFORNIA; NUMBER MC-11 IN EMERALD GREEN. THIS MODEL IS OFTEN FOUND WITH SUN VISORS, FENDER SKIRTS, SPOTLIGHT, AND/OR SUN VISOR. I LIKE IT PLAIN, AS MOST OF THE REAL CARS ON THE STREET WERE UNADORNED IN THEIR DAY. (AUTHOR COLLECTION)

THE CUSTOM DELUXE 1950 4 DOOR SEDAN WAS THE SECOND MOST POPULAR BODY STYLE AFTER THE 2 DOOR SEDAN. THIS PARTICULAR CAR, IN SPORTSMAN'S GREEN AND FITTED WITH AN AFTERMARKET SPOTLIGHT, IS A 1:43 SCALE MODEL HANDCRAFTED IN WHITE METAL BY MOTOR CITY USA, NUMBER MC-15. (AUTHOR COLLECTION)

Ford in miniature

One of the things that makes this Motor City USA scale model 1950 Custom Deluxe so authentic is the builder's attention to detail. Features like the chrome external trunk lid hinges, and layered 'Ford' embossed hubcaps are usually overlooked by manufacturers of lower priced die-cast models. These Motor City USA models of the 1950 Fords were available at retail outlets until the early 1990s. While very detailed and well constructed, they still used traditional detailing techniques such as 'picking out' the windshield wipers in silver paint, or scraping down to bare metal, practices later replaced by photo-etched parts and chrome bare metal foil. (Author collection)

1950 Los Angeles squad car made for the Los Angeles Police Department. Motor City USA model number MC-14P with authentic logos and dashboard-mounted police radio. (Author collection)

A limited edition model; fewer than 300 examples were released by Motor City USA. The maker also issued a police squad car version – number MC-14P – of its 1940 Fordor sedan in the USA line. (Author collection)

This view of Motor City USA's 1950 Ford police patrol car shows the attention to detail. Visible is the black speedometer with white numbers, gear shift with plastic end piece, and nickel-plated driver's window winder. The police radio is just out of sight below the instrument panel. Model number MC-14P. (Author collection)

Ford

1950 Custom top up convertible, fully outfitted with spotlight, fender skirts, and continental wheel. Motor City USA model number MC-10X. (Author collection)

Over 50,000 1950 Ford convertibles were sold in the days before affordable air conditioning arrived; more than half of the Kaiser cars sold that same year. Motor City USA model number MC-10X. (Author collection)

Finished in the popular shade of Osage Green with contrasting tan canvas top, and loaded with extras, in price the Custom convertible was second only to the Country Squire. The Motor City USA model, number MC-10X, pictured here retailed at around $250 when it debuted circa 1990. (Author collection)

1950 Custom 2 door sedan, well equipped with fender skirts and whitewall tires. Motor City USA model number MC-12. (Author collection)

Ford in miniature

As the balance of the post-war sellers' market began to shift toward buyers, Ford introduced, late in the model year, a 2 door sedan to rival the new hardtop convertibles produced by General Motors. Pictured here is a Motor City USA model of the Custom Deluxe Crestliner 2 door sedan next to its plainer 2 door sedan sibling. The Crestliner has the 1951 Mexicali Maroon color with black canvas roof. Of note is that the plainer sedan also sports a 1951 color, Polynesian Bronze, a lighter version of the 1951 Hawaiian bronze color. (Author collection)

Almost 675,000 of these 2 door sedans went to customers by the end of the 1950 model year. During the early days of the 'Baby Boom', 2 door passenger vehicles were popular with young families because they enclosed wayward children in the back seat. Many of today's automobiles have security door locks that make it difficult for children to fall out of a moving vehicle. This was not the case in 1950. Motor City model number MC-12, handmade from white metal. (Author collection)

In total 8703 Custom Deluxe Crestliner 2 door sedans were sold in 1950 versus 76,662 Bel-Air hard tops. Motor City USA model number MC-14. (Author collection)

The 1950 Victoria was essentially a special trim package applied to the 2 door sedan. Intended to mimic the appearance of the 'hard top convertible' of its competitors, the Victoria had a vinyl roof and strategically placed chrome highlights to make the roof appear lighter and convertible-like. It is debatable whether this actually worked but it can be said that the Victoria was a special Ford with appearance touches such as chrome 'rocker panels' and scalloped two-tone side trim not shared by its lesser siblings. Motor City USA model number MC-14. (Author collection)

FORD

1950 CUSTOM DELUXE CRESTLINER 2 DOOR SEDAN. MOTOR CITY USA MODEL NUMBER MC-14. (AUTHOR COLLECTION)

TO ENSURE AUTHENTICITY, MOTOR CITY USA INSTALED FULL WHEEL COVERS ON THIS MODEL, MAKING IT THE COMPANY'S ONLY 1950 FORD SCALE MODEL WITH THIS TREATMENT. MODEL NUMBER MC-14. (AUTHOR COLLECTION)

1951 CRESTLINER 2 DOOR SEDAN FROM USA MODELS, THE JUNIOR LINE OF MOTOR CITY USA. THESE MODELS LACK ONLY EMBLEMS, SCRIPT, AND SOME INTERIOR DETAIL FOUND ON THE 'FULL' MOTOR CITY MODELS WHICH THEY ARE BASED UPON. MODEL NUMBER USA-17. (AUTHOR COLLECTION)

1951 CUSTOM DELUXE OPEN CONVERTIBLE INTERIOR: MOTOR CITY USA MODEL NUMBER MC-52. 'FULL' MOTOR CITY USA MODELS HAVE A VERY HIGH LEVEL OF DETAIL WHICH INCLUDE SUN VISORS, INSIDE REAR VIEW MIRRORS, INDIVIDUAL INSTRUMENTATION, GEARSHIFT LEVERS, HORN RINGS, INSIDE DOOR HANDLES, AND WINDOW WINDERS. (AUTHOR COLLECTION)

AN ALPINE BLUE 1951 CUSTOM DELUXE OPEN CONVERTIBLE. THIS MOTOR CITY USA MODEL NUMBER MC-52 WAS PRODUCED SEVERAL YEARS AFTER THE 1950 MODELS, IN THE MID-1990S, AND USED BARE METAL CHROME FOIL ON THE SIDE MOLDINGS TO GIVE A BRIGHT APPEARANCE TO THE CHROME TRIM. (AUTHOR COLLECTION)

Ford in miniature

1951 CUSTOM DELUXE OPEN CONVERTIBLE AND 1951 VICTORIA HARD TOP COUPÉ. MOTOR CITY USA NUMBERS MC-52 AND MC-51, THESE MODELS WERE INTRODUCED MORE THAN FIVE YEARS AFTER THE 1950 REPLICAS PICTURED EARLIER. AS A RESULT, THEY BENEFITED FROM ADVANCEMENTS IN MODEL-MAKER TECHNOLOGY, NOTABLY THE USE OF BARE METAL FOIL AS OPPOSED TO SILVER PAINT FOR THE BRIGHTWORK. (AUTHOR COLLECTION)

INTERIORS OF EARLY 1950 FORD AUTOMOBILES WERE FAIRLY SIMPLE AND RESTRAINED, WITH HIGHER-END MODELS RELYING ON TASTEFUL, TWO-TONE PAINT AND A FEW CHROME ACCENTS TO PROVIDE AESTHETIC APPEAL. THIS 1:43 SCALE HANDBUILT MOTOR CITY USA VICTORIA ACCURATELY RECREATES THE AUTOMOBILE'S PASSENGER COMPARTMENT. (AUTHOR COLLECTION)

A LIGHT AND AIRY ENVIRONMENT GREETED PASSENGERS OF THE VICTORIA HARD TOP COUPÉ. ALL 1951 FORD MOTORCARS HAD ROCKET-INSPIRED CHROME TAIL LIGHT EMBELLISHERS THAT EXTENDED ALONG THE SIDES. NOTICE ALSO THE ABUNDANCE OF BRIGHTWORK AROUND THE REAR QUARTER PILLAR. THIS MODEL IS FINISHED IN AUTHENTIC HAWAIIN BRONZE WITH A GLOSSY SANDPIPER BEIGE ROOF. MOTOR CITY USA MODEL NUMBER MC-51. (AUTHOR COLLECTION)

IN 1951, FORD BROUGHT OUT THE CUSTOM DELUXE VICTORIA, THE COMPANY'S FIRST HARD TOP, BASED ON THE REINFORCED CONVERTIBLE CHASSIS. IT PROVED VERY POPULAR, WITH MORE THAN 110,000 CARS FINDING HAPPY OWNERS. THAT YEAR, THE CRESTLINER REALLY DID BECOME SIMPLY A HIGHER TRIMMED 2 DOOR SEDAN, WITH 8703 SOLD FOR THE MODEL YEAR. MOTOR CITY USA MODEL NUMBER MC-51. (AUTHOR COLLECTION)

Ford

1951 Deluxe 4 door sedan, Brooklin dealer special number 3. Amongst Brooklin model collectors, the 'dealer special' is a highly coveted prize. Occasionally the builder issues a special model to club members, or to customers who have proof of purchase of other Brooklin models in addition to the money necessary to purchase the model. These models feature unique body styles and colors. Brooklin is particularly effective in marketing its products and has built a loyal customer base. (Courtesy D Mathyssen)

1951 Victoria by Brooklin. This is model BRK-51 from the late 1990s. A sturdy handbuilt with good proportions and a proper roof treatment. Many model-makers start out with a convertible and then add a top to it, thus creating two body styles. If done well, it can be impossible to tell that the hard top is based on the convertible. If done poorly, the sleight of hand is obvious because the top looks awkward; either too large or too small, or ill-fitting, particularly where it meets the windshield header. Brooklin avoided these problems by casting this model as a hard top and not attempting a convertible. (Courtesy D Mathyssen)

A light green 1951 Victoria was the model issued by Brooklin to commemorate the Modelex Show in 1995. 750 of these attractive handmade scale models went to lucky visitors of that event. Number BRK-51X. (Courtesy D Mathyssen)

1951 Deluxe Fordor sedan from Brooklin, model number BRK-51A, in the livery of the San Francisco, California police department. (Courtesy D Mathyssen)

As a fundraiser for victims of the 2001 terrorist attack on New York City, Brooklin issued 200 pieces of this lovely 1951 Fordor sedan in the livery of the New York Fire Department. Model number BRK-51B. (Courtesy D Mathyssen)

Ford in miniature

1951 Fordor sedan in the livery of the Diamond Taxi Company, issued by Brooklin for the Canadian Toy Collectors' Society 1996 Show. Limited to 375 pieces, model number BRK-51. (Courtesy D Mathyssen)

A 1951 Ford dealership in Canada may have featured these models in its showroom: Custom Deluxe convertible, Custom Deluxe Victoria, and Monarch. This photograph is from one of my dioramas "OK Falls Ford", where I display some of my model collection. (Author collection)

Manufactured in Canada, 1949 Monarchs were based on the Mercury Monterey. However, grille, interior fabric, two-tone paint schemes, unique 'lion's head' emblems, and other trim distinguished them from their American cousin. This much in demand model is the 1949 Monarch from Brooklin, number 15F, issued for the Canadian Toy Collectors' Society. (Courtesy D Mathyssen)

1951 Monarch; Durham Classics model number DC-8. This is a chrome trim-detailed Durham Classics, a heavy model at over 1lb/454 grams! (Author collection)

Model-by-model 1952-1956

The 1952 to 1956 period saw the Korean conflict, and a price war between General Motors and Ford that spelled doom for most of the remaining independent automobile manufacturers. For the Ford Motor Company, 1952 marks the organization's return to common styling cues for all lines in an effort to have the 'low-priced' Ford resemble the mid-priced Mercury and premium Lincoln lines. Advances during this period were the Plexiglas roof on Skyliners and a brief foray into safety features, such as padded dashboards and seatbelts included in the optional 'Lifeguard' package on 1956 models. Finally, Ford's retort to rival Chevrolet's Corvette was the Thunderbird, which, of course, became an instant classic.

In the 1:43rd scale handbuilt model world several examples exist of the Thunderbird and only a smattering of 1954-1956 full-sized Ford motorcars. Light trucks from the redesigned 1953 to 1955 period are well represented.

Some of the 'mints' that produce models have a particular penchant for promoting the unique or 'collectible' features of their models. In an effort to increase their market, they fear neither hyperbole nor any unique fact that will contribute to speculative buying behavior. The builders featured in this book seem to be just the opposite. Their exquisite products 'fly below the radar'; produced in small quantities and appreciated by relatively small numbers of knowledgeable collectors.

CONTINUED PAGE 51

1952 F1 PANEL DELIVERY OUTFITTED AS A SAN FRANCISCO AMBULANCE TO COMMEMORATE THE 5TH ANNIVERSARY OF THE SAN FRANCISCO BAY BROOKLIN CLUB. 1 OF 300 PIECES, THIS IS BROOKLIN MODEL NUMBER BRK-42. (COURTESY D MATHYSSEN)

A LIMITED PRODUCTION 1952 F1 LIMOUSINE-STYLE HEARSE BASED ON BROOKLIN MODEL NUMBER 42. 300 WERE MADE IN 2004 FOR MODELLAUTOS BUDIG, A SHOP IN GERMANY. THEY CAME IN A SPECIAL BLACK LEATHERETTE BOX SIMILAR TO THE 30TH ANNIVERSARY SPECIALS. THE MODEL HAS SIDE CURTAINS AND A COFFIN IN THE BACK. (COURTESY D MATHYSSEN)

1952 FORD F1 PANEL TRUCK BY BROOKLIN, MODEL NUMBER BRK-42. 1000 OF THESE MODELS WERE ISSUED IN 1993 WITH ALKA SELTZER LOGO. (COURTESY D MATHYSSEN)

1952 FORD F1 RANGER FROM THE LATE 1990S IN YOSEMITE NATIONAL PARK TIOGA ROAD PROJECT LIVERY. IN RECOGNITION OF THE US NATIONAL PARK SERVICE AND TO COMMEMORATE THE SAN FRANCISCO BAY BROOKLIN CLUB'S 12TH ANNIVERSARY. MODEL NUMBER BRK-42B; LIMITED TO 200 PIECES. (COURTESY D MATHYSSEN)

1950 FORD UTILITY TRUCK IN THE PHONE COMPANY'S LIVERY. THIS HANDBUILT WHITE METAL MODEL IS FROM US MODEL MINT, A LINE THAT IS CARRIED BY BROOKLIN MODELS. MODEL NUMBER 12. (COURTESY D LARSEN)

Ford in miniature

1954 Crestline Victoria hard top coupé, issued by Oakland Models during the mid-1980s. Originally an Auto Buff model based on a master reputed to be from England, the Ford master and parts were sold to Oakland models. (Courtesy D Larsen)

1954 Crestline Victoria hard top. This Oakland Models, resin handbuilt model number 3, has abundant brightwork and detail, including red wheel cover centres. (Courtesy D Larsen)

1954 Crestline Victoria hard top, Oakland Models number 3. The model pictured was built and detailed by Bruce Arnold for the Model Museum collection: Says Bruce: "I acquired the [resin-bodied with stamped metal roof] '54 Ford model in need of restoration. It is still in my opinion, the only acceptable '52-'54 Ford road car obtainable. [Durham Classics offers an exellent sedan delivery] This obsolete model has accurate lines and measures out at exactly 1:43 scale, with the only discrepancy being tail lights that seem a little small. The restored model is painted Sandstone White over Flamingo Orange. Nostalgic miniatures made an all metal (tires too!) 1952 hard top in the 70s that was quite heavy-handed and, of course, Collectors' Classics made a 'limited' number of '53s but, in my opinion, they were not accurately modeled. The Oakland Models '54 Ford is quite rare and sells for around $200 when available. While they are not in the same league as, say, Design Studio and Madison models, I think they are very much worth the time and effort required to find one."

"Though most Oaklands I've seen were supplied with AMT 1:43 kit tires that were reversed and had painted whitewalls, this one came with excellent tires that I have never seen before or since. The dash is good and the rest of the interior is fairly well done, though there is no inner door panel detail. I added a mirror, stalks, winders, handles, arm rests and correct trim to finish off the interior properly". (Courtesy B Arnold)

FORD

1953 Victoria 2 door hard top coupé in Roman Red by Collectors' Classics, the Argentine company that made models in the 1980s. This maker's models have the distinction of being made using the die-cast method and are hand assembled. Detail and materials are very good and certainly not toy-like. This is model number CC-2H. (Author collection)

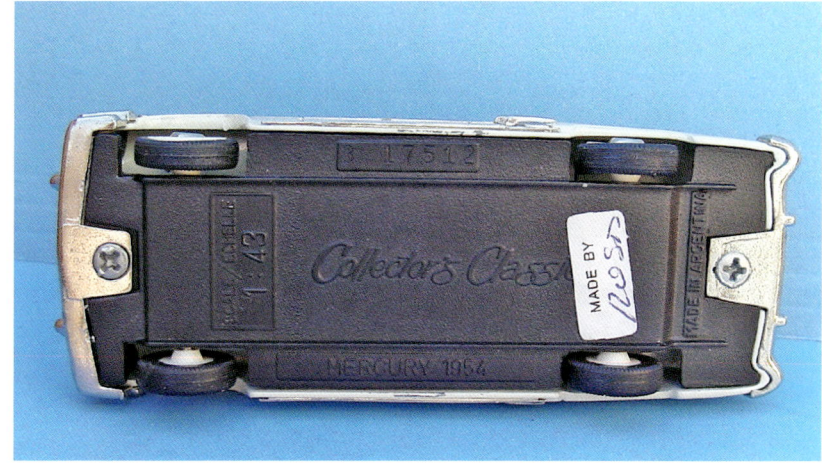

One of the charming features of every Collector's Classics model is the sticker on the base that is hand-signed by the assembler. Here, 'Rosa' has made a nice job of a 1954 Mercury Sun Valley. (Author collection)

The 1954 Ford Courier. 350 of these models were issued by Durham Classics. The actual vehicle upon which the model was based was never registered, nor issued license plates because it was only used at the Avro Aircraft factory. Originally issued in black, the last surviving member of the Avro research team pointed out to Durham Classics that the actual vehicle had been dark blue, which resulted in pieces 176-350 being painted in Avro's correct colors. Model number DC-7. (Author collection)

This 1954 Ford Courier sedan delivery is model number 7 from Durham Classics of Canada. Finished in a glossy Buttercup Yellow, it is a replica of a Colonial Airways company vehicle. (Author collection)

1953 Ford F 100 pickup by Durham Classics, several variations of which were introduced in the 1990s. Known for its brick solid build quality, superb paintwork and finishing, the model was a worthy replica of the actual truck, sharing many attributes with the real thing. This model has a separate drive shaft and an exhaust pipe running underneath. Model number DC-2. (Courtesy A Moskalev)

1953 Ford F 100 pickup. Durham Classics DC-2H. Finished in bright red, it had a spare wheel on the side, authentic Wurlitzer music logo on the doors, and a miniature Wurlitzer jukebox as load. (Courtesy Durham Classics Automotive Miniatures)

1954 Ford pickup (tow truck) finished in light green with white crane and Cities Service gasoline logos on doors. 250 examples were produced. Durham Classics model number DC-24A. (Courtesy Durham Classics Automotive Miniatures)

1955 Ford pickup (tow truck) finished in red with blue crane and Sohio gasoline logos on the doors. 250 examples were produced. Durham Classics model number DC-25. (Courtesy Durham Classics Automotive Miniatures)

FORD

1954 Courier sedan delivery towing a 1932 Ford roadster hot rod. Durham Classics issued this set around 2002 in competition with Brooklin Models' popular 'Racing Weeks' sets which featured a 1952 F1 panel van pulling a competition 'Battlebird' Thunderbird on a trailer. (Courtesy Durham Classics Automotive Miniatures)

1955 Ford panel van in the livery of Pan American Airways. Modeled as a ground support vehicle used by the airline, Durham Classics did careful research to ensure that proper colors were reproduced; hence, the dark blue trim with light blue background and authentic PAA logo. 300 numbered examples were issued in 2003. Model number DC-37. (Courtesy Durham Classics Automotive Miniatures)

1955 Ford panel van. One of the last models issued by Durham Classics in late 2003. Model number DC-37. (Courtesy Durham Classics Automotive Miniatures)

Right: 1955 Sunliner and Crown Victoria Skyliner. In 1955, Ford provided sun-worshippers with the choice of an open air convertible or transparent roofed coupé. With just under 50,000 buyers, the soft top outnumbered Plexiglas models by a ratio of 25 to 1. Motor City USA models numbers MC-28 and MC-16S respectively. (Author collection)

Ford in miniature

Left: 1955 Sunliner and Crown Victoria Skyliner. Motor City USA models, numbers MC-16S and MC-28. (Author collection)

The 1955 Motor City USA Sunliner, number MC-15, was offered in a few color combinations, including solid Raven Black and the prototypical Seasprite Green (turquoise) and white. (Author collection)

The profile of the 1955 Ford Crown Victoria had sculpted chrome moldings reminiscent of the famous 'Darren Dip' of custom-bodied automobiles from the previous two decades. Motor City USA white metal, handbuilt model number MC-16S. (Author collection)

A terrific 1955 Crown Victoria Skyliner MC-16S. Motor City USA also issued this model as a steel-roofed Crown Victoria, model number MC-16. (Author collection)

This stunningly detailed 1955 Georges Pont of France patterned Crown Victoria Skyliner is for CCC's US line. The small French builder brings out a few US models each year, cast in resin and limited usually to just 100 or so pieces. Model number CCCUS-4. (Courtesy D Larsen)

The 'basket handle' 1955 Skyliner Crown Victoria 2 door hard top coupé as modeled by Motor City USA, number MC-16S. (Author collection)

48

FORD

1955 CROWN VICTORIA IN NEPTUNE GREEN, HANDMADE IN WHITE METAL BY MOTOR CITY USA. MODEL NUMBER MC-16. (COURTESY D LARSEN)

RAVEN BLACK SUNLINER MC-15 BY MOTOR CITY USA. THE GRILLE ON THIS MODEL IS EXCEPTIONALLY DETAILED AND REALISTIC-LOOKING; ONE OF THE CHARACTERISTICS THAT OFTEN DIFFERENTIATES A FINE HANDBUILT MODEL FROM LESSER DIE-CAST MODELS. HOW DIFFERENT THE MODEL LOOKS IN ALL BLACK WITH TASTEFUL DARK RED INTERIOR. ALSO ISSUED IN A RARELY SEEN TOP UP VERSION. (AUTHOR COLLECTION)

1955 SUNLINER TOP DOWN CONVERTIBLE. MOTOR CITY USA OF CALIFORNIA ISSUED THIS BEAUTY (NUMBER MC-15) DURING THE LATE 1980S AND EARLY '90S. HANDMADE IN WHITE METAL, IT IS WELL DETAILED AND ACCURATELY PROPORTIONED. IT MAY BE HARD TO TELL FROM THE PHOTOGRAPH BUT THE INTERIOR WINDOW WINDERS AND DOOR HANDLES ARE MOLDED INTO THE DOOR PANELS AND DETAILED IN SILVER PAINT. LATER MODELS FROM THIS BUILDER HAD SEPARATE WHITE METAL PARTS TO REPLACE THE PAINTED DETAILS. THIS ICONIC COLOR COMBINATION – TROPICAL ROSE (PINK) AND WHITE – WOULD HAVE BEEN OUTRAGEOUS JUST A HANDFUL OF YEARS EARLIER. (AUTHOR COLLECTION)

Ford in miniature

Brooklin issued this substantial white metal 1956 Ford Fairlane in Meadowmist Green, model number BRK-23. A somewhat plain model when released, this replica has had much additional work performed on it by John Roberts, who has added chrome moldings, window surrounds and script. 1956 Ford Fairlane, model number BRK-23. (Courtesy D Larsen)

Brooklin produced a dealer special, 1956 Mainline 2 door sedan, model number BRK-23X. (Courtesy D Mathyssen)

Over the years the quality of die-cast models has improved greatly with companies such as Solido, Vitesse, Collectors' Classics, Rextoys, and, of late, Minchamps, issuing nicely proportioned and detailed models. This attractive 1956 Fordor sedan taxicab is from Spain's Altaya Models and can be acquired for $30. Originally outfitted as a taxi cab, a little acetone-based nail polish remover was used to lift off the taxi decals. Some blackwash to the grille and chrome foil applied to the back of the headlights to remove the telltale 'pupil' enabled this model to fit right in with any handbuilt collection. (Author collection)

Left: A vision of 1956 Fords by John Roberts. The artist has enhanced three Brooklin Mainline sedans and one hard top coupé and placed them on a '47 international car carrier/transporter. (Courtesy J Roberts)

FORD

Every so often, a builder will produce a model with a little history, or perhaps even an error. When Durham Classics of Canada issued 1954 Ford Courier sedan delivery models in the livery of the Avro aircraft company in the wrong color, it enclosed a certificate with the models, explaining its apparent error in color choice (as discovered by the last surviving member of the Avro Arrow project team). This helped to build a little interest in newly issued models.

Model-by-model 1957-1959

BRITISH BUILDER MINI MARQUE '43' PRODUCED FOUR BODY STYLES OF THE 1957 FORD. ALTHOUGH THE 1957 CHEVROLET, WITH ITS TAILFINS, IS OFTEN HELD UP AS AN EXEMPLAR OF 1950s STYLING, FORD ACTUALLY OUTSOLD CHEVROLET WHEN IT PREMIERED THE LOW-SLUNG '57s. CLOCKWISE FROM TOP LEFT: DEL RIO STATION WAGON MMQ-19; RANCHERO MMQ-20; SUNLINER MMQ-2B; FAIRLANE MMQ-2D. (AUTHOR COLLECTION)

In North America, the late 1950s were a time of radical automotive design as Chrysler sent General Motors stylists back to their drawing boards to come up with more modern designs for its automobiles. Ford models hold up well in comparison to the low, finned Mopar marvels and the taller GM products of this time. The 1957s and 1959s have a cleanliness and lightness of line that strikes a nice balance between style and utility. The styling of recession year 1958 Fords is often considered a little 'busier' to incorporate the new quad headlights. This, of course, was also the year of Edsel's debut.

All Edsel, Thunderbird, and Ford model body styles from the 1957-59s have been rendered by hand in white metal or resin. 1:43rd scale models of the 1958 and 1959 models made by Western and Brooklin are readily available at your retail source. 1957 models can be obtained through patient surveillance of auctions and re-sellers.

A few words about Ford's famous failed marque. Like the real car, Edsel models have not proliferated in 1:43 scale. Brooklin, Zaugg, Mini Marque '43', and lately, Minichamps have all introduced fine models of the first year 1958s. Western modeled the almost forgotten 1959s. It is hard to say which are the best.

The Citation-based Mini Marque '43' models were produced early in the model-maker's life and lack some of the detail of later models. I like their colors and chrome but they have a very low stance and strike me as being, in a word, 'flat'. Brooklin's is so similar that it makes one wonder if the same patterns were used ... The Zaugg model of the lesser status Pacer is midway between a serious model and a toy with springs like a Corgi. It was about 1:45 in scale. The Minichamps Edsel Bermuda wagon is a faithful reproduction.

Western's 1959 4 door sedan is nicely detailed and is a keeper. Finally, hats off to Brooklin Models for releasing the 1960 Ranger that, no surprise, bears a strong resemblance to its 1960 Ford Sunliner.

CONTINUED PAGE 61

THIS 1957, 2 DOOR DEL RIO, IN A RICH FLAME RED WITH TORCH RED ROOF AND LOWER BODY, IS ONE OF THE RARELY MODELED STATION WAGONS, NUMBER MMQ-19. THE MODEL-MAKER HAS TAKEN LIBERTIES WITH THE TWO-TONE PAINT ON THIS REPLICA, COMBINING THE LATTER COLOR THAT WAS NOT AVAILABLE UNTIL THE 1958 MODEL YEAR. A POPULAR BODY STYLE DURING THE BABY BOOM YEARS, FORD SOLD 106,000 2 DOOR STATION WAGONS IN 1957, ALTHOUGH TWICE AS MANY 4 DOOR WAGONS FOUND BUYERS THAT YEAR. BRITISH BUILDER MINI MARQUE '43' HAS DONE A VERY NICE JOB ON THIS MODEL WITH THE USE OF PHOTO-ETCHED CHROME MOLDINGS THAT HIGHLIGHT THE BODY CONTOURS WITH CLEANLINESS AND PRECISION. THIS IS ONE OF ONLY 50 MODELS ISSUED IN THIS COLOR FOR A COLLECTORS' CLUB IN NEW JERSEY. (AUTHOR COLLECTION)

Ford in Miniature

1957 Sunliner top down convertible. This Mini Marque '43' convertible is quite common by handbuilt standards with a few thousand issued. This is a newer version with separate chrome door handles and photo-etched Fairlane script above the grille. Both of these items were upgrades to the original silver-painted brightwork and decals. This model, in 2000, had a retail price of just under $180. Model number MMQ-2B. (Author collection)

This 1957 Fairlane Club Victoria is a well-detailed replica that includes accurate trim and badges on the continental wheel cover. Model number MMQ-2D. (Author collection)

An attractive, well-detailed, two-tone 1957 Ranchero was issued in white metal by Mini Marque '43' in the 1990s. Builders of handbuilt models tend to aim for realism, and will often put signs on their models of utility vehicles to reflect their commercial use. Model number MMQ-20A. (Author collection)

Usually called a 2 door hard top today, Ford maintained its 'Victoria' title for the pillar-less 1957 Fairlane body style. This Fairlane Club Victoria replica, with two-tone paintwork and continental wheel cover, is Mini Marque '43' model number 2D. The addition of a continental wheel with bumper extensions made the Fairlane Club Victoria somewhat longer than the stock 207.7 inches. This Mini Marque '43' model, number 2D, was also available without the continental wheel. (Author collection)

1957 Ranchero by Mini Marque '43' in Flame Red and Colonial White. A handmade white metal model of more than 70 pieces, including a separate roof. Model number MMQ-20. (Courtesy D Larsen)

1957 RANCHERO. THIS HANDBUILT WHITE METAL MODEL IS FROM BROOKLIN AND WAS PRODUCED IN 2005 WITH THE NUMBER BRK-108. ONCE AGAIN, BROOKLIN MODELS PRODUCED AN AFFORDABLE HANDBUILT MODEL BY SIMPLIFYING THE PATTERN TO REDUCE THE NUMBER OF PARTS REQUIRED. FOR EXAMPLE, THE MINI MARQUE '43' RANCHERO PICTURED PREVIOUSLY HAD A SEPARATE ROOF, TWO-PIECE HEADLIGHTS, AND NUMEROUS TRIM DETAILS WHICH ARE ABSENT ON THE BROOKLIN. RETAILING AT LESS THAN $100, BROOKLIN MODELS WILL SELL AT LEAST 5000 OF THESE UNITS. AT MORE THAN TWICE THE PRICE, MINI MARQUE '43' SOLD JUST OVER 1000 UNITS OF ITS MODEL, PROVIDING PURCHASERS WITH A MORE DETAILED REPLICA. BOTH MODELS ARE EXCEPTIONALLY NICE. (COURTESY D MATHYSSEN)

1957 SKYLINER WITH RETRACTABLE ROOF IN THE ERECTED POSITION. THIS IS THE ONLY HANDBUILT REPLICA OF THE RARE MODEL THAT FOUND 20,766 BUYERS IN 1957. ONLY 544 CUSTOMERS WANTED THIS PALE YELLOW BROOKLIN MODEL NUMBER BRK-35 FROM 1993. (COURTESY P TONDEUR)

A SPECIAL VERSION FOR THE SAN FRANCISCO BAY BROOKLIN CLUB; THE BUILDER CELEBRATED THE BAY AREA'S SURROUNDING WINERIES AND CREATED THIS AUTHENTIC-LOOKING 1957 RANCHERO. BROOKLIN MODELS NUMBER BRK-108. (COURTESY D MATHYSSEN)

CANADA'S VERSION OF THE 1957 MERCURY – AVAILABLE ONLY TO FORD DEALERS – WAS THE MONARCH. THIS SPECIAL EDITION – BROOKLIN MODEL NUMBER BRK-28X – WAS MADE FOR THE CANADIAN TOY COLLECTORS' SOCIETY, AND WAS LIMITED TO 450 PIECES. (COURTESY D MATHYSSEN)

BOTTOM LEFT: IN 1957 IT WAS NOT UNCOMMON FOR AUTOMAKERS TO VARY THE WHEELBASE AND OVERALL LENGTH OF THE ASSORTED MODELS THEY PRODUCED, EVEN WITHIN THE SAME LINE. OF THE FOUR MODELS PICTURED, THE LONGEST WAS THE FAIRLANE CLUB VICTORIA AT MORE THAN 220 INCHES WITH THE CONTINENTAL WHEEL EXTENSION. THE RANCH WAGON WAS SHORTEST AT 203.5 INCHES. THE WHEELBASE OF THE STATION WAGON, AT 116 INCHES, WAS ALSO 2 INCHES SHORTER THAN THE SEDAN, CONVERTIBLE, AND VICTORIA. EACH OF THESE MINI MARQUE '43' MODELS IS AROUND 5 INCHES IN LENGTH. PICTURED LEFT-RIGHT: RANCHERO (NUMBER MMQ-20); FAIRLANE CLUB VICTORIA (NUMBER MMQ-2D); DEL RIO RANCH WAGON, AND SUNLINER OPEN CONVERTIBLE (NUMBER MMQ-2B). (AUTHOR COLLECTION)

A rare 1954 Thunderbird prototype with Fairlane-inspired side trim that was not adopted by Ford when the T-Bird debuted in 1955. Durham Classics brought out this lovely handbuilt replica in a very limited run during 2002. The heavy white metal model from the Canadian builder has the same excellent proportions as its Brooklin counterparts, but features a little more detailing, and a chrome, one-piece windshield surround that greatly enhances the model's overall appearance. (Courtesy Durham Classics Automotive Miniatures)

Ford Motor Company's Thunderbird became an instant classic when it was introduced for the 1955 model year. As was to be expected, several toy and model manufacturers issued replicas of the company's landmark design. In handbuilt form, Brooklin Models rendered this well-proportioned 1:43 scale white metal model, number BRK-13. It enjoyed a long production run in standard form from 1987 to 1994, and in many custom variations such as this version with white metal Omen figure of Marilyn Monroe made for the Deutschland Club. A long-standing Brooklin offering, the 1957 replica, is still readily available from stockists. (Courtesy D Mathyssen)

1955 Thunderbird convertible in Raven Black, a Code 2 replica sanctioned by Brooklin Models, Dean Paolucci's DMP Studios of Canada rendered just 100 of these stunning, glossy black, open 1955 convertibles. Based on Brooklin Models' handbuilt white metal model number 13, in addition to the lustrous paintwork and careful chrome detailing, Dean added delicate photo-etched wire wheels with knock-off hubs to create a very special replica. (Photo by Don Markle; model courtesy D Paolucci)

Ford

1957 Ford Thunderbird top down in white metal with open rumble seat. Made especially for the Canadian Toy Collectors' Society in 1996. 1 of 230 issued; model number BRK-13ax. (Courtesy D Mathyssen)

1958 Thunderbird Tudor hard top coupé in Silvertone Blue and Colonial White from A&S, model number 1. This handbuilt, white metal British model from early 1990 is well-proportioned with a very high level of detail and craftsmanship. The 'squarebirds' have also been issued by Brooklin, Mini Marque '43', ELC, Belgium Trucks, and Jupiter Models. (Author collection)

The author's 1957 model number 16 from the Conquest Models line. This Colonial White and Starmist Blue model features a top with porthole windows and windwing-type vent windows. It is completely detailed down to the engine-turned metal dash inserts. Model number CNQ-16. (Author collection)

A&S Models of England issued beautiful 1:43 scale handbuilt white metal models such as these 1958 Thunderbird hard top and open convertibles. A&S model number 1. (Author collection)

What a differnce a year makes! Ford Motor Company's decision, after only three model years, to produce the Thunderbird as a four passenger model was regarded by some as folly. However, it was a smart business move that resulted in a significant sales increase for the high margin marque, and ensured the 'classic' status of the two-seater. Accurate in proportions, color, and every trim detail, the two models depicted here are the finest 1957-58 Thunderbird replicas produced in 1:43 scale. 1958 Thunderbird tudor hard top coupé in Silvertone Blue/Colonial White by A&S Models, and 1957 Thunderbird with porthole top in Starmist Blue/Colonial White by Conquest. (Author collection)

1958 Thunderbird open convertible finished in authentic Gulfstream Blue from A&S. Model number 1. (Author collection)

Ford in miniature

1958 Thunderbird top down convertible. A&S Models of England crafted this terrific white metal model number 1. Details include the hood-mounted winged bird emblem and authentic chromed Thunderbird script at the leading edge of each front fender. (Author collection)

1958 Thunderbird convertible by A&S. Note the interior treatment, including door handles, window winders, and chrome steering wheel horn ring. Mini Marque '43' also produced a convertible and hard top using the former A&S patterns. (Author collection)

1959 Thunderbird Tudor hard top coupé by Brooklin Models, number BRK-64 in maroon. (Courtesy D Mathyssen)

1959 Thunderbird Tudor hard top coupé by Brooklin Models, number BRK-64 in Powder Blue. (Courtesy D Mathyssen)

1959 Thunderbird open convertible by Brooklin Models, number BRK-64A. (Courtesy D Mathyssen)

FORD

1959 T-Bird Convertible 'Chinese New Year Parade' made in 2002 for SFBBC. 1 of 200. Model number BRK-64ax. (Courtesy D Mathyssen)

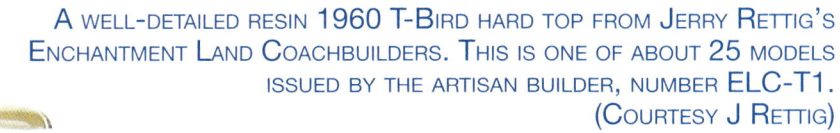

A well-detailed resin 1960 T-Bird hard top from Jerry Rettig's Enchantment Land Coachbuilders. This is one of about 25 models issued by the artisan builder, number ELC-T1. (Courtesy J Rettig)

Left: These two late '50s Fords were issued as handmade white metal models in the mid-1990s and are up-to-date in their use of photo-etched trim materials and high-quality paint finish. Their smooth, shiny white metal headlights, whilst not out of place on a replica, would likely be replaced today by the more common two-piece white metal and clear resin headlamps used by most builders. 1958 Thunderbird by A&S Models and 1957 Ranch Wagon by Mini Marque '43'. (Author collection)

Left: 1958 Sunliner issued by Marque One Models of England. Crafted in resin, it has a very realistic grille and trim. Available as both open and top up versions. numbers 7 and 8, and as a Victoria 2 door hard top, number 9, these models sometimes become available at auction or at antique shops and hobby stores. Expect to pay around $100. (Author collection)

1958 Sunliner top up convertible by Marque One Models, number 8. (Courtesy J Rettig)

Ford in miniature

Though not considered an artistic success, the 1958 Ford sold quite well in a recession year. This 1958 Ford Custom 300 sedan by Western Models Ltd was an accurate and carefully constructed and finished replica of a popular motorcar found throughout North America. This replica is based on the personal vehicle of Western Models' Mike Stephens who remarked to me that it was a terrific, smooth-running automobile with the 6 cylinder engine. Model number SW-17. (Courtesy Western Models Ltd)

Here's the taxi version of the 1958 300 sedan by Western, model number SW-17T. (Courtesy Western Models Ltd)

1958 Edsel Citation 2 door hard top coupé in Flamingo Pink. Handcrafted in white metal by Brooklin Models. Discontinued in 1992; model number BRK-22. (Courtesy D Mathyssen)

Top: 1958 Edsel Citation 2 door hard top coupé with continental wheel. One of three standard models issued over the years in different colors, this is the third version introduced in green. Brooklin Models number BRK-22. (Courtesy D Mathyssen)

Middle: 1958 Edsel Citation 2 door hard top coupé in Ember Red. In 1991, 500 replicas were handbuilt for the UK Brooklin Collectors' Club. (Courtesy D Mathyssen)

Bottom: Part of the Brooklin Video Set II, this nice, white and red 1958 Edsel Citation convertible is one of 450 pieces issued worldwide. Even rarer is the black and red number at 50 pieces. Model number BRK-22x. (Courtesy D Mathyssen)

FORD

1958 Edsel Pacer convertible by Zaugg, the Swiss company which made several white metal Ford Motor Company replicas. This handbuilt 1:43 scale model is number 8C in its line. (Courtesy J Rettig) Inset: 1958 Pacer 2 door hard top. Zaugg also made this hard top version of the mid-range Edsel. Zaugg's model had accurate proportions and was moderately detailed. It even had spring suspension that is very unique for a handbuilt model. The scale was closer to 1:45 than 1:43. Model number 8. (Author collection)

1958 Citation 2 door hard top in profile. One of the things that contributes to the high price of a handbuilt model is the extraordinary level of detail necessary to make it an accurate copy of the original motorcar. In this case, Mini Marque '43' chose to reproduce the insignia and emblems and the huge, rocket-shaped molding inside the rear fender concavity. Model number MMQ-5B. (Author collection)

1958 Bermuda station wagon by Minichamps in celebration of Ford Motor Company's centenary. The company issued several thousand of these die-cast models at around $50 apiece. Not a handbuilt, but still nice, and the only readily available 1:43 scale model Edsel station wagon. (Author collection)

Mini Marque '43' model number 5A is a top down 1958 Edsel Citation convertible finished in white and red. This 1:43 scale model was handbuilt by SMTS for Mini Marque '43' in England. (Author collection)

Mini Marque '43' issued a 1958 Citation hard top 5B that looks striking in black and red with the silver-colored rear fender insert. One of the last Edsel models available at the time of Richard Briggs' death, founder of Mini Marque '43'. The author paid $180 for this model in 2002. (Author collection)

1959 Edsel Corsair 4 door sedan, the most popular top line Edsel for 1959. even so, only a meager 3301 units were sold. Western Models introduced this well-detailed and accurately rendered replica, number WMS-89, around 2000. The company has enjoyed a proud tradition of modeling less common cars, and this Corsair certainly qualifies in that respect. Priced at around $150, only a few hundred have been issued in two colors: the yellow and grey seen here, and brown and white. (Author collection)

Ford in miniature

1959 Skyliner retractable from Western. This is an earlier casting that was a little too wide. Later models have better proportions and detail, reflecting Western Models' commitment to accuracy. Model number 46. (Author collection)

Ford's popular 1959 models have been rendered in 1:43 by Western Models' Small Wheels line: number SW-21. The beauty here, finished in Geranium, is the Fairlane 4 door sedan, which features enamel headlight lenses, a highly-detailed blackwashed grille, photo-etched wipers and side trim, chrome door handles, and colorful badges. Modelers usually use red foil over the white metal parts to depict taillights. This is an effective way of providing color and a reflective appearance. The alternative material is plastic, which usually deteriorates after a decade or two. Cost-saving measures include script decals and no vent windows. As Western competed with its neighbor, Brooklin, vent windows were gradually introduced on successive models. (Author collection)

1959 Sunliner open convertible by Western Models, an earlier scale model from this company that has quite a high level of exterior detailing. Note that the rear lower bodyside molding is a large separate piece. The many parts that go into a handbuilt white metal model such as this add greatly to its complexity, cost, and ultimately, rarity. Model number WMS-46. (Courtesy Toys for Collectors USA)

1959 Country Squire station wagons. These great-looking models from Western feature realistic-looking wood appliqués with contrasting trim. A superb rendering of Ford's top-of-the-line people carrier, model number 82. (Courtesy Western Models Ltd)

60

FORD

1959 COUNTRY SQUIRE STATION WAGON BY WESTERN. WOODY WAGONS ARE POPULAR WITH COLLECTORS. ORIGINALLY ISSUED IN WHITE AND BLACK, THIS SLATE BLUE MODEL IS A 2005 ADDITION TO WESTERN MODELS' LINE-UP OF HANDBUILT MODELS. MODEL NUMBER WMS-82. (COURTESY TOYS FOR COLLECTORS)

Brooklin Models' 2005 release of the 1963 Falcon convertible is available at many outlets.

CONTINUED PAGE 64

1960 SUNLINER CLOSED CONVERTIBLE BY BROOKLIN. MODEL NUMBER BRK-37 IN ORCHID GREY (METALLIC LAVENDER). DISCONTINUED IN 1998. (AUTHOR COLLECTION)

1959 RETRACTIBLE FROM FRANKLIN MINT. AN EXCEPTIONALLY WELL-DETAILED DIE-CAST MODEL WITH SEVERAL OPERATING FEATURES; THIS IS MODEL NUMBER 50-14. (COURTESY J RETTIG)

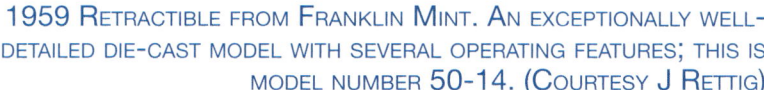

Model-by-model 1960-1963

By the early 1960s the majority of independent automakers on the North American scene had all but disappeared. Chrysler was in trouble as its 1961-1962 Dodge and Plymouth models flopped. The full-sized and intermediate Galaxie and Fairlane were solid competition to the General Motors products, and the Falcon and Thunderbird led their market segment.

Modelers of handbuilts have paid little attention to this period, with the exception of the 1960 and 1963 full-sized Ford and the Falcon and Thunderbird. 1960 Edsel and Galaxie models from Brooklin Models may still be available at your stockist, as may be the nice 1961 and 1963 Thunderbird made by Tin Wizard.

1960 SUNLINER OPEN CONVERTIBLE; A CODE 2 CONVERSION BY DEAN PAOLUCCI'S DMP STUDIOS OF CANADA. AUTHORIZED BY BROOKLIN, ONLY 75 OF THESE LOVELY RED MODELS WERE ISSUED. AS CAN BE SEEN, DEAN'S WORK IS FABULOUS AND INCLUDES CAREFULLY APPLIED CHROME DETAILING ON THE SCRIPT, AND BODY EDGES SUCH AS THE FINS AND DOOR TOPS. (COURTESY DEAN PAOLUCCI)

Left: This white 1960 Edsel Ranger open convertible and a black Ranger, both with red interior, were sold as part of a limited edition set by Brooklin Models in 1998. (Courtesy D Mathyssen)

Main pic: 75 of these 1960 Sunliners by DMP Studios were also made in blue. This model has blackwall tires and non-standard wheel covers. Details like these make it a very unique and realistic model. DMP Studios issued a small number of 1955 T-Birds in black and a 1950 Mercury convertible in red. (Courtesy Dean Paolucci)

Right: 1960 Ranger open convertible by Brooklin. Model number BRK-75. This is the only 1960 1:43 scale model of this automobile. (Courtesy D Mathyssen)

Ford's compact Falcon model, introduced for the 1960 model year, has been modeled in 1:43 scale by several builders. This Canary Yellow and White 4 door sedan is the nicest and rarest of the lot. Handmade in white metal by Milestone Miniatures, it is model number 2. 2006 value would be around $200. (Courtesy J Rettig)

Falcon Sprint 2 door hard top by Brooklin, introduced during the mid-1990s. Model number BRK-58. (Courtesy D Mathyssen)

FORD

1963 Falcon Futura Sports convertible, Brooklin model number BRK-112 issued in February 2005. Compared to Brooklin's earlier hard top coupé, the increased chrome detailing is evident: door handles; windshield frame and wipers; side-spear molding; rear ornament, and blackwashed grille. This handmade white metal model was good value at around $90. (Courtesy D Mathyssen)

Above: 1963 Falcon station wagon with full woodgrain trim. This die-cast replica is produced by Trax of Australia which also introduced the model in 4 door sedan and pickup (ute) configuration. It is a model of the Australian car with right hand drive and barely noticeable shorter rear overhang from the North American version (2in less on the actual car to reduce the frequency of vehicles being hung up on uneven road surfaces in the Outback). This is the only replica in this scale of a Falcon wagon, which makes a good companion to the North American models in a Falcon collection. (Courtesy J Rettig)

1963 Falcon 2 door hard top Provence Moulage. A resin model, number 877, that was handbuilt and detailed by Bruce Arnold for the Model Museum collection: "Compared to the Brooklin version, the Provence Moulage Falcon has all the right handbuilt touches; photo-etch trim, full color decals and a less heavy-handed look. It can be built stock or as a racer. Provence Moulage is out of business and this kit is becoming harder to find." – Bruce Arnold. (Courtesy J M Arnold)

A highly detailed 1963 Country Squire station wagon in Corinthian White from Conquest, model number CNQ-9. It appeared in 1991. Because it was issued in such small numbers and is a highly coveted 'Woody' wagon, it rarely appears for sale in the aftermarket. Beside it is a 1963 Ford Galaxie 500 open convertible in Heritage Burgundy Metallic. SMTS handcrafted this lovely white metal model in 1990 for Fa. Daimler House's Conquest Models (model number CNQ-4C). The 1963 Galaxie 500 replica was also available as a 2 door hard top (model number CNQ-4). SMTS later issued several competition versions with full race paraphernalia. (Courtesy J Rettig)

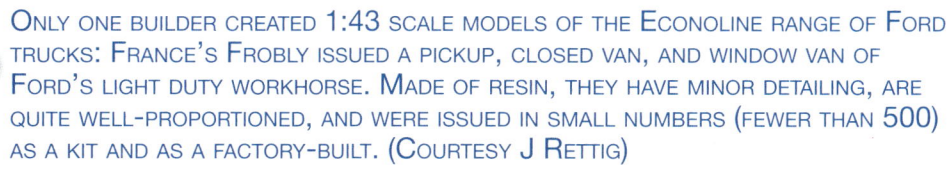

Only one builder created 1:43 scale models of the Econoline range of Ford trucks: France's Frobly issued a pickup, closed van, and window van of Ford's light duty workhorse. Made of resin, they have minor detailing, are quite well-proportioned, and were issued in small numbers (fewer than 500) as a kit and as a factory-built. (Courtesy J Rettig)

Ford in miniature

1961 Thunderbird Indianapolis 500 pace car in gold. The sleek, redesigned Bird was a fitting choice to pace that year's race. Tin Wizard model number TW-508. (Courtesy Tin Wizard)

1961 Thunderbird pace car. Ford made sure that its pacer was up to the task with three Holley 2 barrel carburetors atop a 390 cubic inch Thunderbird Special to power this boat. Tin Wizard model number TW-508. (Courtesy Tin Wizard)

Model-by-model 1964-1969

Perhaps the most exciting North American automobile to be introduced in 1964 was Ford's Mustang, which captured the imagination of a large cross-section of purchasers and was a sales success throughout the sixties.

It will come as no surprise that Ford's pony car has been a favorite of modelers of handbuilt 1:43rd scale models. More Mustangs have been issued in white metal and resin than any other Ford for this time period. In fact, only one full-sized Ford, not one Falcon, and only one 1968 Torino/Fairlane (from Milestone Miniatures and Toys For Collectors) have been rendered.

Brooklin Models has seen fit to issue 1965 and 1967 Thunderbird replicas which are still available. Enchantment Land Coachbuilders may still build you a 1965 T-Bird; Western Models makes a nice 1965 Mustang convertible, and Brooklin's 1968 Mustang fastback is still sold at stores.

1963 Thunderbird hard top coupé by Tin Wizard. French company, Provence Moulage, once produced a resin body 'transkit' version to be used in converting a Solido die-cast model to a hard top. Tin Wizard produces the complete model and it is the best available. A nice replica, number TW-505-1. (Courtesy J Rettig)

1964 Galaxie 2 door hard top by Road Champs. This die-cast has been detailed with bare metal chrome foil. There is a large gap in availability of handmade early 1960s models of full-sized Fords, with only Conquest/SMTS issuing the 1963 model. (Courtesy J Rettig)

1966 Galaxie 4 door hard top by Dinky Toys. A die-cast model that has received some light detailing, this is a faithful replica of the popular family motorcar. (Courtesy J Rettig)

More than 140,000 full-sized, 1964 Country Squire and Country Sedan station wagons were manufactured but only one maker chose to model this popular motorcar in the scale shown. That maker was AMT which sold a few thousand polystyrene kits. Few are built up as nicely as this example. (Courtesy J Rettig)

FORD

1966 Ford Galaxie 4 door hard top manufactured by Model A Automodelli of Brazil. Labeled as a '1967 Ford Galaxie'. Available colors: white, blue and burgundy; two-tone blue with white top and burgundy with black top are also available. Model was recently released in stretched limousine and ambulance forms. This era Ford Galaxie was very popular in Brazil and remained unchanged for several years. Model A Automodelli was founded in 1999 by Antonio Apuzzo, and is based at a toy shop in São Paulo, Brazil. Builder Bruce Arnold notes: "There are some proportion issues but it's good to see new companies making a contribution to the hobby. Most trim is accomplished with photo-etch, including the exterior door handles. There are few cast or plated trim parts where we would normally expect them but considering these are unique Brazilian models that coincidently have an exact American counterpart, we can't complain too much. Look for more crossovers from Model A Automodelli in the future." (Courtesy J M Arnold)

1967 Thunderbird Landau 4 door sedan. Brooklin model number 92. (Courtesy D Mathyssen)

1965 Thunderbird convertible, handmade in limited numbers by Jerry Rettig of Enchantment Land Coachbuilders. (Courtesy J Rettig)

1969 Thunderbird, 1:43 scale AMT polystyrene model handbuilt by master builder, Bruce Arnold. (Courtesy J M Arnold)

1968 Thunderbird 2 door hard top by Sabra/Cragstan. The Hong Kong toy maker produced this die-cast model from the late 1960s to early 1970s. (Courtesy J Rettig)

Ford in miniature

Another 1969 Thunderbird 2 door hard top from AMT. This polystyrene model was built from a kit. (Courtesy J Rettig)

1965 Mustang top down convertible in green and 1965 Mustang notchback in red. Precision Miniatures produced these well-proportioned models in white metal during the early 1980s which are typical of the better-detailed replicas being made at that time. Model numbers 18 and 22. (Courtesy J Rettig)

1965 Mustang Pace car in white metal. Brooklin Models Factory Special from 1994. 1 of 2000 issued; model number BRK-56X. (Courtesy D Mathyssen)

Precision Miniatures also issued these handbuilt white metal 1965 Shelby GT 350 and Shelby Daytona versions, numbers 20 and 21. (Courtesy J Rettig)

1965 Mustang convertible in white metal by Brooklin Models, number BRK-56. (Courtesy D Mathyssen)

1966 Mustang notchback by Starter. Resin, built up from a kit. (Courtesy J Rettig)

FORD

1968 Mustang, model number BRK-24. This white metal model was a gift from John Hall of Brooklin Models to Mike Stephens of Western Models. Only one was made in this light metallic green color. (Courtesy D Mathyssen)

1966 Fairlane 2 door fastback by Matchbox. A nicely-detailed and accurately proportioned die-cast model that is still quite plentiful on the aftermarket. (Courtesy J Rettig)

1968 Mustang GT500 convertible from Danbury Mint's Classic Sports Cars Series. Made from pewter. (Courtesy J Rettig)

'Bullitt'. A Shelby-ized 1968 Mustang fastback from Brooklin, number BRK-24X, for the Brooklin Club Deutschland in 1994. 1 of 250. (Courtesy D Mathyssen)

Another high quality handbuilt is Western Model's version. This white metal replica has a number of details found only on better models: photo-etched windshield wipers; separate chromed door handles; 'Ford' script on the hood and sun visors, to name but a few. 1965 Ford Mustang Convertible by Western Models, number WMS-80. (Courtesy Toys for Collectors USA)

This 1968 Torino 2 door fastback is an inexpensive die-cast model from Sabra. It would require much detailing to blend in with the Matchbox 1966 Fairlane die-cast or handmade offerings issued during the past decade or two. However, it has good proportions and an acurate-looking front clip that takes it out of the 'toy' category. (Courtesy J Rettig)

1965 Ford Mustang Convertible by Western Models. Rallye lights in the grille enhanced sportiness and perception of higher value of the '60s Mustangs. Model number WMS-80. (Courtesy Western Models Ltd)

67

FORD IN MINIATURE

1968 FORD TORINO FASTBACK BY AMT, BUILT AND DETAILED BY BRUCE ARNOLD. SAYS BRUCE: "SOME OF THE AMT 1:43 SCALE SERIES WERE MODELS OF CONTEMPORARY, CURRENTLY AVAILABLE AUTOMOBILES, MAKING THESE EXTRAORDINARILY ACCURATE SNAP-KITS POPULAR WITH ALL AGE GROUPS. WHEN HIGHLIGHTED WITH CHROME FOIL, THIS 1968 TORINO SHOWS ALL THE DETAIL OF A REAL FORD. THOUGH AMT RE-ISSUED THESE KITS IN THE EIGHTIES AND AGAIN IN THE NINETIES, THE ONLY OTHER PLASTIC KIT MANUFACTURER TO RELEASE A 1:43 SCALE MODEL WAS MONOGRAM (WHICH PUT OUT A BEAUTIFUL 1967 VETTE CONVERTIBLE KIT COMPLETE WITH MANY PHOTO-ETCH PARTS). UNFORTUNATELY, THIS EXCELLENT MODEL NEVER FOUND ITS NICHE AND MONOGRAM SCRAPPED PLANS TO RELEASE A SIMILAR KIT OF THE 1967 FORD MUSTANG." (COURTESY B ARNOLD)

LEFT: 1970 TORINO GT FROM ERTL. THIS INEXPENSIVE DIE-CAST MODEL FROM CHINA HAS BEEN WELL-DETAILED BY JERRY RETTIG. WHILE THE MAKER HAS DONE A GOOD JOB REPLICATING THE FRONT CLIP, THE REAR TREATMENT IS SOMEWHAT INACCURATE. (COURTESY J RETTIG)

ABOVE & LEFT: 1970 TORINO GT FROM ERTL. (PHOTOS COURTESY J M ARNOLD; MODEL COURTESY B ARNOLD)

Lincoln 3

Handbuilt Lincolns cover mostly the 1938-1964 time period.

Summary of major models

The '30s

Aside from a few pewter and die-cast 1920s and 1930s Lincolns, Durham Classics (Canada) crafted the first significant handbuilts, beautiful coupé and convertible 1938 Zephyrs. Recently, Brooklin (UK) issued a '38 Zephyr sedan.

Seven model years of Lincoln motorcars from 1951-1957. From left to right: 1957 Premiere from Madison, number MAD-8; 1956 Premiere also Madison, number MAD-2; 1955 Capri from Motor City USA, number MC-65; 1952 Capri from Motor City USA, number MC-74, and 1951 Cosmopolitan, again from Motor City USA, number MC-34. (Author collection)

The '40s

The Continental of the 1940s caught the fancy of many more than just *The Godfather's* Sonny Corleone. Several builders spawned 1940s Continentals, including a 1946 pace car and convertible from Collectors' Classics (Argentina) and 1940-41 convertibles and coupés from Rio (Italy), Enchantment Land Coachbuilders (USA), and Collectors' Classics. The regular old Lincoln was largely ignored until 2003, when Western (UK) released a nice '48 4 door sedan which was followed by a 2 door sedan in 2005.

The '50s

Three 1:43 scale handbuilt white metal models from Motor City USA. Left to right: 1951 Cosmopolitan top up convertible, number MC-34; 1952 Capri 2 door hard top coupé, number MC-74, and 1955 Capri 2 door hard top coupé, number MC-65. (Author collection)

'Bathtub Lincolns' were Brooklin's '49 Cosmopolitan top down and Fa. Daimler House's (Holland) 1950 sedan, and Motor City USA's 1951 Cosmopolitan convertible.

The Mexican road racecars are well represented with hardtop and convertible models for 1952-53, and 1955 from Precision Miniatures (USA), Motor City USA, BBR (Italy), and Western.

Even the Batmobile 1956-57s are replicated by Fa. Daimler House and Brooklin (in 2003).

There are a couple of sedate, tasteful 'Connies' from 1956, and even more of the humungous 1958-60 boats made by Brooklin, Legendary (USA), and Mini Marque '43' (UK).

Ford in miniature

The '60s

Kennedy year Lincolns exist in Mini Marque '43's nicely detailed 1964 sedan. Legendary closed out the decade with a finely crafted 1969 Lincoln Continental Mark III as depicted in the hit Hollywood movie, *The French Connection*.

Model-by-model — 1930-1939

For North American automobiles, the 1930s were a time of great advances, especially streamlining of car bodies. In tune with the design changes of this period, Ford Motor Company's flagship brand introduced the aerodynamic Zephyr. Its advanced styling presaged all Ford model styling for the next few years.

If a 1:43rd scale model of a 1930s Lincoln is what's required, choice is confined to the 1938-39 Zephyr (with the exception of, perhaps, 25 resin handbuilt models of the 1932 Lincoln roadster from Enchantment Land). A careful search of stores and auctions may yield a Durham Classics 1938 convertible or coupé. More readily available, as of 2004, is Brooklin Models' 1939 Zephyr sedan.

PRE-1930S: 1927 LINCOLN MODEL L OPEN ROADSTER, A PEWTER REPLICA FROM DANBURY MINT. DANBURY MINT PRODUCED SEVERAL 1:43 SCALE MODELS DURING THE 1980S AND EARLY 1990S BUT AS OTHER 'MINTS' AND HANDBUILT MAKERS INTRODUCED MODELS, DANBURY SWITCHED EMPHASIS TO 1:24 SCALE MODELS. (COURTESY J RETTIG)

PRE-1930S: THIS 1929 LINCOLN TOP DOWN PHAETON IS BELIEVED TO BE A CLAUDE THIBIVILLIER CONVERSION OF RIO MODELS' DIE-CAST VERSION. MON. THIBIVILLIER UNDERTOOK MANY CONVERSIONS DURING THE EARLY 1980S AND IS REGARDED AS A MASTER CRAFTSMAN WITH FINISHING TECHNIQUES SECOND TO NONE. IF THIS IS A THIBIVILLIER MODEL IT IS AN EXTREMELY RARE AND VALUABLE ITEM BECAUSE OF ITS EXCEPTIONAL QUALITY. (COURTESY A THOMAS)

LINCOLN REPLICAS FROM THE EARLY 1930S ARE RARE. ENCHANTMENT LAND COACHBUILDERS MADE MODEL NUMBER L-12, A CHARMING RENDITION OF THE 1932 LINCOLN ROADSTER INDIANAPOLIS PACE CAR. (COURTESY J RETTIG)

PRE-1930S: A 1927 LINCOLN TOWNCAR 'JUDKINS'. OBVIOUSLY A SKILLED CONVERSION OF A DIE-CAST MODEL, OR POSSIBLY DANBURY MINT PEWTER MODEL, THIS IS A ONE-OF-A KIND REPLICA. (COURTESY A THOMAS)

1937 ZEPHY 2 DOOR SEDAN. THIS RARE MODEL IS A ONE-OFF, HANDMADE IN RESIN BY ANDREW THOMAS OF LINCOLNS DOWNUNDER. IT USES COMPONENTS, SUCH AS THE BUMPER AND GRILLE, FROM A DIE-CAST MATCHBOX MODEL. (COURTESY A THOMAS)

1938 Lincoln Zephyr coupé. Durham Classics, number DC-4. (Courtesy D Larsen)

Two shots of a magnificent one-of-a-kind model of the 1940 Lincoln Zephyr with coachwork by Brunn, the 'Beaver Tail' formal sedan as used by Mrs Henry Ford Snr. John Roberts made extensive modifications to a white metal Brooklin Zephyr 4 door sedan to create this unique model. (Courtesy J Roberts)

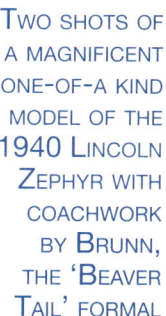

1938 Lincoln Zephyr 4 door sedan in Eagle Grey Metallic by Brooklin Models, number BRK-106. This is the standard version issued in 2004. (Courtesy A Thomas)

John Roberts re-painted and enhanced Brooklin's 1938 Lincoln Zephyr 4 door sedan to make a one-of-a-kind white metal model. (Courtesy D Larsen)

1941 Lincoln Continental convertible with top up. This is a mystery model from the author's collection that was acquired as a 'throw in' from a fellow collector. It is made from resin and has a metal base. The finish is a little rough, suggesting that it was made by an amateur modeler. However, the detail is quite good and it may, in fact, be an earlier version of a rare Enchantment Land Coachbuilders model, or perhaps an Elegance model, which were made in France and are quite scarce. The author has decided to keep it because it looks pretty nice and is intriguing. (Author collection)

Model-by-model 1940-1948

As motorcars became more affordable and commonplace, fewer extravagantly priced, custom bodied Darrin or Derham type automobiles occupied the roads of North America. Recognizing that a market still existed for luxurious, more individualistic motorcars, Lincoln introduced the stylish Continental. Face-lifted for the post-war market, Continentals bore a strong resemblance to the rest of the Lincoln family.

Continental models were very popular with producers of both die-cast and handbuilt models in 1:43rd scale. They should be available in a range of price ranges at retail outlets and on the aftermarket. The only non-Continental 1940s Lincoln is the Western Models attractive, mid-priced 1948 4 door sedan that was issued in 2003.

Ford in miniature

ABOVE: 1941 Continental open convertible rendered in pewter by Danbury Mint. (Courtesy J Rettig)

BELOW: 1941 Continental coupé. Enchantment Land Coachbuilders, number L-1. Jerry Rettig built approximately 25 of these attractive resin models, further enhanced by the red wheels. (Courtesy J Rettig)

1946 Continental, specially designed and built for designer Raymond Loewy. A Brooklin 'dealer special' in dark green. Brooklin model number DS-X2. (Courtesy A Moskalev)

1946 Continental for designer Raymond Loewy. Brooklin Models issued this handbuilt 'dealer special'. Even rarer is a version that Century Models of France produced (not pictured). Whilst more delicate than the Brooklin around the griille area, the British version is more accurate. (Courtesy A Moskalev)

1941 Long Wheelbase Continental limousine. Handmade resin model from Enchantment Land Coachbuilders. (Courtesy J Rettig)

LINCOLN

1948 LINCOLN SEDAN. THE COMPANY SOLD A LITTLE OVER 6400 LINCOLN MODELS IN ALL THREE BODY STYLES DURING THIS TRANSITION YEAR. WESTERN MODELS ISSUED THIS NUMBER 83 IN 2003. THE MODEL HAS EXCELLENT PROPORTIONS, TERRIFIC EXTERIOR DETAILING, AND SCALES OUT ACCURATELY TO 1:43 OF THE SIZE OF THE ORIGINAL. ITS INTERIOR HAS SOME DETAILING, PARTICULARLY THE BUTTON TUFTING TO THE SEATS AND AN EMBOSSED BEIGE DASHBOARD. AN EXCELLENT MODEL FOR A MODERATE PRICE OF $150. (COURTESY D LARSEN)

1946 CONTINENTAL. THIS STATELY GRAY COUPÉ IS A RESIN HANDBUILT MODEL FROM VENERABLE FRENCH BUILDER PROVENCE MOULAGE. A MODEL THAT WAS OFFERED IN THE LATE 1980S AND EARLY 1990S IN BOTH KIT AND BUILT UP FORMS, IT IS QUITE SCARCE TODAY. THE DETAILING IS FABULOUS. REGARD THE SCRIPT ABOVE THE FENDER AND THE TWO-TONE LEATHER-LIKE UPHOLSTERY TEXTURE. THE MODEL IS COMPRISED OF MANY PARTS. A WORTHY COMPONENT OF ANY HANDBUILT AND/OR DIE-CAST MODEL COLLECTION. (COURTESY J RETTIG)

1948 LINCOLN 2 DOOR SEDAN, HANDMADE IN WHITE METAL BY WESTERN MODELS. USING MANY OF THE SAME COMPONENTS AS THE 4 DOOR SEDAN, THIS ALL-NEW BODY STYLE MADE ITS DEBUT IN 2005. IT IS THE ONLY ISSUED 1:43 SCALE LINCOLN OF THIS BODY STYLE AND 1946-48 PERIOD. (COURTESY WESTERN MODELS LTD

Model-by-model   1949-1951

The so-called 'Bathtub Lincolns' introduced in 1949 were quite a departure from the maker's previous models. Similar in shape but more cleanly styled than Packard cars of the same era, they outsold all of their rivals except for Cadillac; the 73,000-plus units sold boosted sales tenfold compared to the previous year.

Three different producers of handbuilt 1:43rd scale models chose the larger 1949-1951 Cosmopolitan series as subjects for their replicas: Motor City USA and Conquest models, which were produced in the 1990s, are hard to find, but Brooklin Models' 1949 Cosmopolitan convertible was still available as of 2006.

1950 COSMOPOLITAN SEDAN FROM CONQUEST OF HOLLAND. MODEL NUMBER CNQ-10 IN NASSAU BEIGE METALLIC AND CARLSBAD TAN. HANDBUILT IN 1992, IT IS A SEDAN WITH A SOMEWHAT SQUAT APPEARANCE. (COURTESY D LARSEN)

1948 LINCOLN 4 DOOR SEDAN, MODEL NUMBER 83 FROM WESTERN MODELS LTD. (COURTESY WESTERN MODELS LTD)

ABOVE: 1949 COSMOPOLITAN PRESIDENTIAL CONVERSION OF A WHITE METAL BROOKLIN, MODEL NUMBER 94, BY ANDREW THOMAS. (COURTESY A THOMAS)

Ford in miniature

1949 Cosmopolitan long wheelbase convertible; two views of a special model. Presidents Harry Truman and Dwight Eisenhower had a stretched version of the Cosmopolitan, complete with continental wheel and 'bubble top' – a clear roof section at the rear. The roof section was removable for dry days when the automobile became a suitable parade car for the head of state. John Roberts used two Brooklin 1949 Lincoln convertibles in this conversion to the presidential parade car. Though missing the continental wheel, this conversion has a set of rear-facing seats and the duplicate chrome 'eyebrow' over the rear wing/fender, just like the original. (Courtesy D Larsen)

1949 Cosmopolitan convertible, Brooklin number 94. Though less expensive than the Conquest sedan, Brooklin Models managed to give its model a more elongated appearance by placing the headlights further apart. A well-proportioned, quality replica. The top up convertible is a John Roberts conversion as Brooklin did not issue any top up models. (Courtesy A Thomas)

A grey 1949 Cosmopolitan convertible was released by Brooklin Models in July, 2002, model number BRK-94. (Courtesy D Mathyssen)

A pair of 1951 Lincoln Cosmopolitan convertibles in Avon Blue and Chantilly Green. Motor City USA model number 34. (Author collection)

1949 Lincoln Cosmopolitan open convertible by Brooklin Models, number BRK-94. (Courtesy D Mathyssen)

1951 Lincoln Cosmopolitan top up convertible. This rear view shows how well outfitted the Lincoln was: note the dual back-up lights, chrome trimmed rear window, and painted and embossed script in the bumper. Model number MC-34. (Author collection)

LINCOLN

NOTICE THE DETAILS; ESPECIALLY THE PINS ON THE WINDSHIELD HEADER FOR FASTENING THE TOP. THESE 1951 COSMOPOLITAN CONVERTIBLES BY MOTOR CITY USA WERE ALSO AVAILABLE IN MAROON. (AUTHOR COLLECTION)

It is easy to forget that the Lincolns of 1952-1955 were very capable, roadworthy automobiles, intended by Ford Motor Company product planners to rival the higher end Oldsmobile and Buick models of the time, although not Cadillac. At this they were well suited and won many road races, especially a series of Pan Americana Mexican events, not to mention the heart of Tom MaCahill, the pre-eminent auto tester of the time. He had a Lincoln as his personal vehicle.

Soon to be known as the 'Hot Rod Lincoln', the prestigious models depicted here featured powerful, high revolution engines, good handling suspension, beautiful color coordinated interiors, and high build quality.

With the exception of 1954, handbuilt replicas from 1952-55 were made by four companies. As of publication date, they are still available from BBR Models and Western Models.

A 1951 CONTINENTAL CONCEPT CAR, TOTALLY SCRATCHBUILT, FROM THE FERTILE MIND OF LINCOLN AFFICIANADO, ANDREW THOMAS. (COURTESY A THOMAS)

CAPRI 2 DOOR HARD TOP COUPÉS FROM THREE DIFFERENT BUILDERS: MOTOR CITY USA MODELED THE RED AND WHITE '52 COUPÉ; PRECISION MINIATURES CREATED THE EMERALD AND WHITE '53 EXAMPLE AT CENTRE, AND BBR OF ITALY HANDCRAFTED THE RESIN '52 MODEL IN AMETHYST AND WHITE AT OUTSIDE RIGHT. (AUTHOR COLLECTION

1952 WITNESSED A DRAMATIC STYLING CHANGE IN THE LINCOLN. THESE TWO CONVERTIBLES BEAR LITTLE RESEMBLANCE TO EACH OTHER, EVEN THOUGH THEY'RE PART OF THE SAME FAMILY. THE BLUE 'BATH TUB'-STYLE LINCOLN IS A 1951 AS MODELED BY MOTOR CITY USA. THE BLACK OPEN NUMBER ON THE RIGHT IS A 1953 MODEL 'ROAD RACE' LINCOLN FROM THE SAME COMPANY. (AUTHOR COLLECTION)

THE MOST APPARENT DESIGN DIFFERENCES ARE BETWEEN THE AMETHYST BBR MODEL AND THE OTHER TWO. THE BBR PATTERNMAKER WAS CARLO BRIANZA; DICK ARMBRUSTER MADE THE PRECISION MINIATURES AND MOTOR CITY USA PATTERNS. DETAIL SUBTLETIES LIKE THE CUT LINES OF TRUNK LIDS, SHAPE AND DETAILING OF TAILLIGHTS, AND THICKNESS AND CURVATURE OF BUMPERS, COMBINE TO CREATE SLIGHTLY DIFFERENT-LOOKING MODELS. ALL ARE EXQUISITELY CRAFTED. (AUTHOR COLLECTION)

Model-by-model 1952-1955

A FAVORITE SUBJECT, THREE COMPANIES HAVE MODELED THE 'ROAD RACE' LINCOLNS. HERE ARE (LEFT TO RIGHT): 1952 AND 1953 LINCOLN CAPRIS FROM MOTOR CITY USA, MODEL NUMBERS MC-75D AND MC-74, AND PRECISION MINIATURES NUMBER 231. (AUTHOR COLLECTION)

Ford in Miniature

1953 Lincoln Capri, Motor City USA's MC-75D top down convertible. Although often called 'conservative', a careful examination of the 1952-55 Lincoln models will reveal many subtle features that placed them a notch above the competition, including the Oldsmobile 98 and even the Cadillac Series 62. Along with the Hudson, the Lincoln was the best handling automobile of this period, thanks to the MacPherson ball-joint suspension. The car's physical appearance was light and understated with subtle trim; it also had one of the cleanest instrument panels of the decade. Interior colors, fabrics, and patterning coordinated effectively with all other components in the package. (Author collection)

This Precision Miniatures 1953 Lincoln Capri was handcrafted in the 1970s. Pictured, from the author's collection, is a special model that has been detailed by pattern maker, Dick Armbruster. Model number 231. (Author collection)

A rear view of Motor City USA's magnificent 1953 Lincoln convertible, model number MC-75D. (Author collection)

A rare closed 1953 Capri open convertible by Precision Miniatures, number 232, produced from the late 1970s to mid-1980s. (Courtesy A Thomas)

"Dick Armbruster made the master for this Lincoln at a time when pattern makers were still sorting out how to make a model appear symmetrical. Aided by a larger scale dimensioned drawing he found in a radio controlled model magazine, he artfully created a wooden master using the specailly laminated block method that he employed throughout his pattern making career. Bumpers and all smaller pieces were expertly shaped from brass. The end result is a masterpiece.

"This is widely recognised as one of the best of his early Precision Miniature series. Dick deeply cares about his creations and it really shows in the Lincoln. All trim was either foiled or plated at Gene Parrill's Precision Miniatures workshop. This model looks so real that one could mistake a photo of it for the real car at first glance. The interior has full door panels, correct upholstery patterns, and an excellent dash and steering wheel. Nothing is missing outside, either. Decals are accurate and hood and trunk ornaments are made to scale; in fact, there is nothing the least bit heavy-handed anywhere.

"This surely set a new standard in the minds of many other pattern makers. Dick said that you know when you get them just right and that's the way he felt about the Lincoln. Any of Dick's models, such as the wonderful and diverse pieces created for Durham Classics, are important contributions to the hobby, but this is an Armbruster classic."

(Quote courtesy Bruce Arnold as condensed from an article in the esteemed collector publication, *Model Auto Review* – Publisher, Rod Ward)

LINCOLN

1953 Capri by Precision Miniatures. While boxed handbuilt models rarely command the 40-50 per cent premium over loose models that Dinky Toys and Corgi Toys do, the black PMI box is much sought-after for its appearance. (Author collection)

Interior detail of Motor City USA's 1952 Capri. The L David Ash designed instrument panel has been reproduced well in this replica. (Author collection)

1953 Capri 2 door hard top coupé modeled by Motor City USA, model number MC-74. Rarely have 1:43 scale models achieved this level of accuracy. (Author collection)

Two versions of the Road Race Lincoln Capri hard top as patterned by Dick Armbruster. The Regal Red and white 1952 hard top coupé is Motor City USA model number 74. Produced in the early 1990s, it is essentially the younger sibling of the Precision Miniatures Lakewood Green and white model number 231 issued in the late 1970s. (Author collection)

Compare the profile of this green 1953 Capri by Precision Miniatures from the 1970s with the red Capri photograph. The '53 has its side windows in the raised position with the glass frame detailed in. Its vac-formed windows are not quite as smooth as those of the newer Motor City USA model. (Author collection)

The photograph of this red 1952 Capri by Motor City USA 1952 shows the three window sections, the smoother surface of the vac-formed windows, and the body-colored wheel trim rings that were added to the 1990s issued replica. (Author collection)

Ford in miniature

BBR USUALLY MODELS EUROPEAN MOTORCARS. HOWEVER, CARLO BRIANZA CAREFULLY CRAFTED THIS 1952 CAPRI, NUMBER 17A. BBR ALSO MADE 1953 AND 1954 MODEL YEARS, NUMBERS 17E & 17L. EXQUISITELY CRAFTED IN RESIN, THE MARKET PRICE WAS AROUND $300. (AUTHOR COLLECTION)

The Carrera Panamericana was consistently won by Lincoln, hence the term 'Road Race Lincolns' for the models from the 1952-55 time period. The race was actually not run in 1955 or thereafter. It is fun to contemplate how the futuristic but heavier and more luxuriously-sprung 1956 Lincoln model would have fared with the competition. Many of the photographs and models shown here are from Andrew Thomas, creator of what is appropriately billed as "The world's greatest Lincoln model car collection on the web" aka www.LincolnDownUnder.com.

CONTINUED PAGE 83

THIS CLOSE-UP SHOWS THE INSTRUMENT PANEL OF THE 1952 CAPRI MODELED BY BBR. THE BUILDER HAS DONE A CREDITABLE JOB OF REPLICATING THE DASH AND INSTRUMENTATION, BUT HAS TAKEN SOME ARTISTIC LICENSE WITH THE STEERING WHEEL. COMPARE THIS WITH THE MOTOR CITY USA CAPRI MODELS AND IT IS EASIER TO APPRECIATE HOW THE MODELS FROM CALIFORNIA HAVE ACHIEVED THEIR UNDISPUTED REPUTATION FOR ACCURACY. (AUTHOR COLLECTION)

THIS '52 CAPRI FROM BBR MAKES GOOD USE OF MODERN PHOTO-ETCHING TECHNIQUES TO ACHIEVE PRECISE, MINUTE DETAILS SUCH AS THE LINCOLN SCRIPT AND ORNAMENTATION ABOVE THE BUMPER. (AUTHOR COLLECTION)

ANOTHER PAIR OF CARRERA PANAMERICANA RACE MODELS FROM LINCOLN DOWNUNDER. (COURTESY A THOMAS)

1953 CAPRI WITH HISTORICALLY ACCURATE MARKINGS AS IT WAS DRIVEN IN THE MEXICAN CARRERA PANAMERICANA RACE FROM 1952-54. THIS STYLING MODELS REPLICA IS FROM BBR AND IS BASED ON THE STOCK CAPRI PICTURED PREVIOUSLY. (COURTESY A THOMAS)

LINCOLN

1953 SPEEDSTER. A ONE-OF-A-KIND MODEL, CREATED IN WHITE METAL BY LINCOLN DOWNUNDER. (COURTESY A THOMAS)

THE 1952 COSMOPOLITAN SEDAN WON ITS CLASS IN THE 1952 MOBILGAS ECONOMY RUN TEST WITH AN AVERAGE FUEL CONSUMPTION OF 17.2 MILES PER GALLON OVER 497 MILES OF MIXED DRIVING; A VERY GOOD PERFORMANCE FOR ITS DAY. ANDREW THOMAS CREATED THE MODEL PICTURED. IT IS THE ONLY HANDBUILT 1952-53 LINCOLN SEDAN IN EXISTENCE! (COURTESY A THOMAS)

1952 LINCOLN CAPRI 2 DOOR HARD TOP COUPÉ IN RED AND WHITE NEXT TO ITS LIGHTLY FACE-LIFTED 1955 COUNTERPART IN A JAUNTY YELLOW AND BLACK. MODELS BY MOTOR CITY USA. (AUTHOR COLLECTION)

KING HUSSEIN OF JORDAN RODE TO HIS CORONATION IN A 1953 LINCOLN CAPRI SPECIAL CUSTOM CONVERTIBLE. NOTICE THAT THE VEHICLE WAS FITTED WITH OPTIONAL LOWER BUMPER ROAD LAMPS. A MODEL BY ANDREW THOMAS OF WWW.LINCOLNDOWNUNDER.COM. (COURTESY A THOMAS)

TO CELEBRATE FORD'S 50TH ANNIVERSARY IN 1953, LINCOLN PRODUCED THIS ONE-OFF MASTERPIECE. WITH MORE THAN $4000 WORTH OF GOLD APPLIED TO MOST METAL PARTS, THE BODY WAS OF FROST WHITE PEARL ESSENCE. ANDREW THOMAS CREATED THIS SCALE MODEL. (COURTESY A THOMAS)

A pair of 1955 Capri models from Motor City USA. (Author collection)

1955 Capri open convertible from Motor City USA in Hunter Red with contrasting black leather upholstery trim and black roof and top cover. (Author collection)

Lincoln gave its models a restrained restyling in 1954 with a slightly more massive appearance, largely carried over into the 1955 model year. Despite the absence of a 'panoramic' or 'wrap-around' windshield used in the very different looking 1956 Lincoln, the '55s were beautiful motorcars. 1955 Capri models from Motor City USA in Hunter Red, Sunstone Yellow, and Galway Green, atop the distinctive Motor City USA box. The convertible is model number MC-64 and the hard top MC-65. These models were issued by the Southern Californian builder in the early 1990s and released again in 2002 for $275 apiece. (Author collection)

Is it possible that the detail and finishing of the interior of this 1955 Capri open convertible from Motor City USA exceeds that of the earlier 1952-53 models issued by the same builder? Judge for yourself. This un-retouched and greatly enlarged photograph picks out specks of dust on the upholstery and shows the flawless smooth finish of the 1:43 scale handbuilt white metal model. (Author collection)

Another view of the red '55 Capri open convertible from above. Motor City USA, model number MC-64. (Author collection)

ABOVE: 1955 Capri 2 door hard top coupé model from Motor City USA in Sunstone Yellow with complementary black top, model number MC-65. This photograph shows the long rear deck of the 1955 model. Though Lincoln did not make much of it, quite a bit of luggage would fit inside. (Author collection)

The 1954 and 1955 Lincoln models had the obligatory, pointed 'Dagmar' bumper extensions shared by Cadillac and Buick, although these were more restrained than those of their competitors. Motor City USA, model number MC-65. (Author collection)

ABOVE: This Motor City USA model, number MC-64, must rate as one of the builder's best. 1955 Capri 2 door top up convertible handbuilt in white metal to a precise 1:43 scale. (Author collection)

Amongst the explosion of colors that appeared on automobiles in the mid-1950s, green was quite popular. Not the subdued army drab greens or olives of the war years, but the vibrant Galway Green of this 1955 Capri hard top. Oh, and make it metallic, if you can. MC-65. (Author collection)

In this photograph it is just possible to see the two-tone interior and decorative trim pieces that hide the seams of the rear seat leather upholstery. Lincoln motorcars were renowned for their smooth ride and passenger comfort. Soon, however, these chair height seating positions would be replaced by less comfortable postures demanded by lower automobile silhouettes. (Author collection)

Ford in miniature

Comin' at ya! A pair of 1955 Lincoln Capri 2 door hard tops by Motor City USA, lovingly photographed by Lincoln collector, Andrew Thomas. Model number MC-65. (Courtesy A Thomas)

1955 Capri open convertible in Cashmere Coral with two-tone interior. Western Models handbuilt number 74X. (Courtesy A Thomas)

1955 Capri hard top coupé by Western Models, number WMS-74. While its competitors were experimenting with two-tone and even three-tone paint combinations on various body parts, Lincoln used primarily two-tone paint with one color for the body and a complementary or contrasting color for the roof. Pictured here is the authentic Palomino Buff and white combination. (Courtesy Western Models)

LINCOLN

1955 Capri open convertible in red with two-tone interior. Western Models handbuilt model number 74X. (Courtesy Western Models Ltd)

Model-by-model 1956-1957

1955 Futura dream car as modeled by Great American Dream Machines. Never seen on the street, Lincoln's experimental model caused a sensation when it was unveiled at auto shows. Its twin Plexiglas bubbles over the driver and passenger seats never saw the light of day, but many styling cues from this 19ft boat appeared in Lincoln's 1956 and 1957 models. (Courtesy D Larsen)

Left to right: 1956 Premiere by Madison, number MAD-2; 1955 Capri by Motor City USA, number MC-65; 1952 Capri by Motor City USA, number MC-74, and 1951 Cosmopolitan Motor City USA, number MC-34. (Author collection)

The 1956 and 1957 Lincoln took dead aim at General Motors' Cadillac. Some argue that the target should have been the artistically and commercially successful 1957 Imperial by Chrysler, but annual sales of around 40,000 units meant the model more than held its own against the Mopar product. With styling inspired by the 1955 Futura show car, later actually used as television's Batmobile, the Lincolns from this period were very modern and luxurious.

The 1955 Futura dream car was so modern that it was used a decade later as the basis for the Batmobile on television's popular *Batman* series. Great American Dream Machines also released a Batmobile replica in full 'Bat Garb' that proved popular. (Courtesy D Larsen)

Ford in miniature

Today, these actual motorcars are quite rare and the same may be said of the 1:43rd scale replicas. Only Fa. Daimler House produced models of the 1956 convertible and sedan as well as the 1957 sedan. Issued in white metal as part of the Madison line between 1988 and 1991, these models occasionally appear on the aftermarket. Fortunately, Brooklin Models released a 1956 Premiere 2 door hardtop coupé in 2003 that is still in stores.

1956 Premiere replica by Madison, number MAD-5 from 1991. (Courtesy A Thomas)

1956 Premiere convertible with top up in Wisteria; Madison model number MAD-5U. One of the more popular models issued by the Dutch builder, the Madison line of models, was intended as a mid-priced competitor to Western Models. Consequently, early Madison models – such as the 1956 Lincolns depicted here – lacked interior detail such as window winders and door handles. During this transitional period decals were often used instead of photo-etched metal for emblems and insignia. As time went on, builder SMTS and patron/distributor Fa. Daimler House blended together the Madison and higher priced Conquest lines and produced fully detailed – albeit pricier – models. (Courtesy D Larsen)

John Roberts removed the roof and painted and detailed Brooklin's 1956 Premiere to create an exceptional model. This Fairmont Blue model, number BRK-99, has received more than $100 worth of customization to bring it to this level. (Courtesy A Thomas)

In 2002, Brooklin issued model number 99, a nicely proportioned yellow and white 1956 Premiere that has a realistic blackwashed grille and an oversized windshield frame. While the pattern has obviously been painstakingly crafted by a brilliant pattern maker, this replica begs for more detailing to match the heavily chromed original. (Courtesy D Mathyssen)

A later version of Brooklin's 1956 Premiere in Amethyst and White. Model number BRK-99. (Courtesy D Mathyssen)

LINCOLN

A PAIR OF 1956 PREMIERE 4 DOOR SEDANS. NO 4 DOOR HARD TOP SEDANS WERE MADE BY LINCOLN THAT YEAR. PRODUCTION OF 2 DOOR HARD TOP (IE PILLAR-LESS) SEDANS AND 4 DOOR SEDANS WAS ROUGHLY EQUAL AT AROUND 24,000 UNITS EACH. THESE HANDMADE WHITE METAL MODELS, CRAFTED BY SMTS FOR HENK VAN ASTEN'S FA. DAIMLER HOUSE, ARE FROM 1988-89 AND ARE NUMBER 2 IN THE MADISON LINE. (AUTHOR COLLECTION)

1956 PREMIERE 4 DOOR SEDAN BY MADISON. THIS PROFILE SHOWS THE ACCURACY OF THE PATTERN MAKER'S EYE AND THE EXCEPTIONALLY AUTHENTIC-LOOKING PAINTWORK. THE ONLY FEATURE THAT, IN THIS CLOSE-UP, SUGGESTS THIS IS A SCALE REPLICA IS THE SCRIPTWORK. THE BUILDER HAS CAREFULLY APPLIED THE CORRECT GOLD 'PREMIER' AND 'LINCOLN' SCRIPT DECALS. THE USE OF TWO-DIMENSIONAL DECALS TO REPRESENT THREE-DIMENSIONAL SCRIPT HAS LARGELY BEEN REPLACED ON HANDBUILTS BY ACTUALLY MOLDING SCRIPT INTO THE MODEL'S PATTERN, A LA BROOKLIN, OR BY GLUEING PHOTO-ETCHED SCRIPT ONTO THE BODY AS CONQUEST AND MOTOR CITY USA DO TODAY. MADISON MODELS NUMBER 2. (AUTHOR COLLECTION)

1956-1957 are also the years of the classic Continental Mark II. Much has been written about this exclusive and stylistically restrained motorcar. Compared to the great majority of gaudy, chrome-laden North American automobiles that debuted in 1956, the Continental is a world apart. The Continental has been rendered as a handbuilt by Brooklin Models (out of production but obtainable), and lately as a high quality die-cast replica from Minichamps.

CONTINUED PAGE 88

1956 PREMIERE 4 DOOR SEDAN FROM MADISON. IN CONTRAST TO THE BROOKLIN MODELS MADE MORE THAN 10 YEARS LATER, THIS PREMIERE HAS QUITE A BIT OF DETAILING. THE SEATS ARE TWO-TONE, WITH INSERTS IN CONTRASTING COLOR TO THE LARGER SEAT BASE. THIS EXTRA DETAIL COMES AT A COST AS THE MADISON MODELS WERE ISSUED AT CLOSE TO THREE TIMES THE PRICE OF THE BROOKLIN MODELS. PRODUCTION WAS AROUND ONE-FIFTH THAT OF THE UK MAKER'S OUTPUT. MODEL NUMBER MAD-2. (AUTHOR COLLECTION)

1956 PREMIERE 4 DOOR SEDAN REAR THREE-QUARTER VIEW. THE CHROME WINDOW SURROUND IS NICKEL-PLATED WHITE METAL AND IS ACTUALLY CAST AS A SEPARATE PIECE. THE GAP BETWEEN THE WINDOW SURROUND AND ROOF IS VISIBLE IN THIS PHOTOGRAPH. MADISON MODELS NUMBER 2. (AUTHOR COLLECTION)

1957 CONTINENTAL MkII; THE STANDARD VERSION WITH TWO-TONE INTERIOR ISSUED BY BROOKLIN MODELS IN 1993. BROOKLIN MODELS ISSUED THE MAJORITY OF 1956-57 MkIIS IN THE HANDBUILT MODEL MARKET. NOSTALGIC MINIATURES RELEASED A FEW EXAMPLES IN 1:48 SCALE. THIS IS BROOKLIN'S MODEL NUMBER 11. (COURTESY D MATHYSSEN)

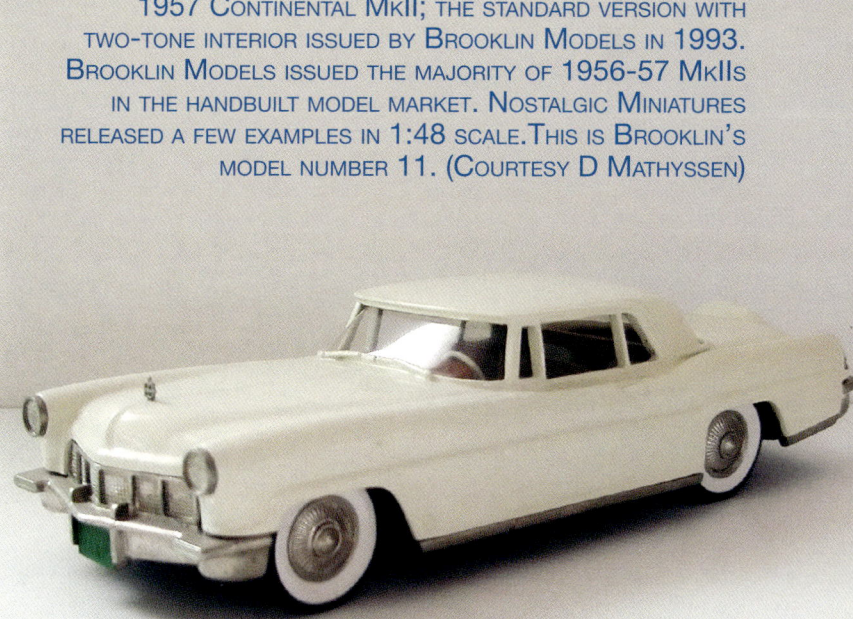

Ford in miniature

1957 Continental MkII. Brooklin Models second standard verion number 11 from 1996. (Courtesy D Mathyssen)

1956 MkII hard top coupé in Cinnamon (metallic red). The rarest and best-detailed handbuilt 1:43 scale MkII ever came from Joel Dickson's Legendary Motorcars. This photograph is from Legendary's promotional brochure in the collection of noted Lincoln collector, Andrew Thomas. (Courtesy A Thomas)

1957 Continental MII by Brooklin Models. One of 25 issued for Auto-Satisfaction of France. Model number BRK-11. (Courtesy A Thomas)

Brooklin Continental MkII. Lincoln created two actual prototypes of the 1957 Continental Mark II convertible. Alas, these were to be the only two because financial considerations intervened to curtail all MkII production by the end of the 1957 model year. A popular scale model, especially with collector clubs, Brooklin Models issued several hundred beautiful MkII convertibles. This pair was sold by Brooklin as a set. As one of only 192 issued it is quite unusual. Model number BRK-11A. (Courtesy A Thomas)

1957 MkII open convertibles in Starmist White (pearlescent white) and Horizon Blue (sky blue) from Legendary Motorcars. Only 15 convertible and hard top models were issued by the company, making them scarce and extremely desirable. This photograph is from Legendary's promotional brochure in the collection of noted Lincoln collector, Andrew Thomas. (Courtesy A Thomas)

86

LINCOLN

1956 die-cast Continental MkII by Minichamps, from the Heart and Soul series to commemorate Ford's centenary. (Author collection)

1957 Premiere 4 door hard top sedan from Madison, model number 8 atop the blue box from Fa. Daimler House. (Author collection)

Two views of Madison Models 1957 Premiere 4 door hard top sedan in Dubonnet Metallic and Flamingo (a very pale pink), and 1956 Premiere 4 door sedan in Brown and white show the influence of the Futura show car and other competitors' finned wonders, particularly Chrysler. In these white metal replicas the pattern makers have reproduced the twin bumper exhaust ports that were eliminated by Lincoln in subsequent years because of their disastrous propensity to corrode and rust out the surrounding chrome bumper. Model numbers MAD-8 and MAD-2. (Author collection)

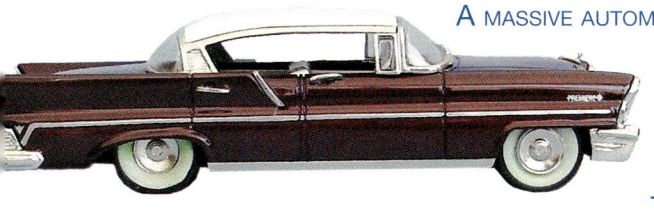

A massive automobile at 4538lb, the 1957 Premiere was still several hundred pounds lighter than its successor. This white metal replica tips the scales at 13 ounces. Madison Models number 8. (Author collection)

The seldom seen 1957 Premiere Landau by Madison, number 8 from 1993, in Horizon Blue and Starmist White. The other color available for Madison's replicas of the 1957 Premiere 4 door hard top sedans was Sand. While Lincoln chose to employ flamboyantly styled sheet metal with chrome accents, Madison used subdued pastel colours on many of its motorcars. (Courtesy D Larsen)

Ford in Miniature

Model-by-model — 1958-1960

Regarded by some as a massive 'land yacht' that was out of step with the times, the Lincoln was actually quite tasteful compared to its Cadillac counterpart. Powered by a mammoth 430 cubic inch motor, the big Lincoln accommodated six passengers in spacious comfort and could consume great lengths of superhighway for days, between fill-ups, of course. But who worried when gasoline was just over twenty cents a gallon?

A fondness for this vehicle has led three makers to render handbuilt models of it, ranging from Legendary Motorcars' ultra exclusive replicas priced at $250-$300; the somewhat more common but out of production, Mini Marque '43' at $200-$250, and the best bet for availability, Brooklin Models' version at under $100.

1960 LINCOLN CONTINENTAL MKV TOP DOWN CONVERTIBLE. THIS REPLICA IS HIGHLY DETAILED AND CRAFTED SUPERBLY IN ENGLAND BY ILLUSTRA FOR LEGENDARY MOTOR CARS LLC. (MODEL 1B). JOEL DICKSON OF LEGENDARY MOTORCARS SAYS THAT THIS WAS A VERY EXCLUSIVE MODEL. ONLY 127 EXAMPLES OF THIS CONVERTIBLE AND A HARDTOP COUPÉ WERE ISSUED. (COURTESY A THOMAS)

1959 CONTINENTAL MKIV TOP DOWN CONVERTIBLE FROM MINI MARQUE '43'; A WELL-PROPORTIONED AND DETAILED WHITE METAL REPLICA FROM THIS UK PRODUCER. ONLY 100 EXAMPLES OF THIS COLOR WERE ISSUED. THIS IS MODEL NUMBER MMQ-36. (COURTESY A MOSKALEV)

1959 CONTINENTAL MKIV TOP UP CONVERTIBLE. IN 2001, MINI MARQUE '43' LISTED THE OPEN CONVERTIBLE AT $195. FOR AN ADDITIONAL $10 THIS SCARCER TOP UP VERSION, FINISHED HERE IN WHITE OVER CAMEO ROSE, COULD BE PRUCHASED. (COURTESY A THOMAS)

1960 LINCOLN CONTINENTAL MKV 2 DOOR HARD TOP COUPÉ. HANDCRAFTED IN WHITE METAL BY LEGENDARY MOTORCARS, THIS GLEAMING BEAUTY IS THE ONLY 1:43 SCALE, HANDBUILT, 1960 LINCOLN HARD TOP ISSUED BY A MODEL MAKER. (COURTESY A THOMAS)

LINCOLN

1960 CONTINENTAL MKV TOP UP CONVERTIBLE FROM BROOKLIN MODELS, NUMBER BRK-57. (COURTESY D MATHYSSEN)

Model-by-model — 1961-1969

The beautiful Elwood Engel-inspired Lincoln Continental from this period has a timeless design and purity of form seldom captured by any automobile maker. Mini Marque '43' hand-rendered this model in white metal in both 4 door hardtop and convertible forms. Century Models did the same with the 1965 version. Both builders' models are obsolete and hard to come by. Every so often one becomes available as part of an estate sale, or from an enthusiast selling their collection.

Despite the fact that Mark IV and V Lincoln models were produced years earlier, the elegant 1968-71 Continental Mark III was declared by many observers a worthy successor to the Mark II. A short decked, long hood 'personal luxury car' with many of the styling cues of its 1956 predecessor, the Mark III was a commercial success. A small number of carefully handbuilt Legendary Motorcars models of the 1969 Mark III were available from Legendary Motorcars LLC, and a few select retailers as this book went to press.

1960 CONTINENTAL MKV TOP UP CONVERTIBLE, A FACTORY SPECIAL FROM 2000 BY BROOKLIN MODELS. MODEL NUMBER BRK-57X. (COURTESY D MATHYSSEN)

1961 LINCOLN CONTINENTAL TOP UP CONVERTIBLE BY BRUCE ARNOLD. SAYS BRUCE: "THIS IS THE SECOND MODEL I CREATED FOR MODEL MUSEUM COLLECTION. THIS CLASSIC CONTINENTAL FEATURES PHOTO-ETCHED FRONT AND REAR GRILLES, A REAL LEATHER INTERIOR, AND A FABRIC ROOF. THERE ARE ACTUALLY ONLY THREE EXAMPLES. ONE IS BEING STORED WITH MY OTHER PATTERNS. ONE WAS SOLD FOR $5000, AND THE ONE PICTURED IS CURRENTLY ON DISPLAY AT THE MODEL MUSEUM IN CALIFORNIA." (COURTESY B ARNOLD)

TWO VIEWS OF A 1960 CONTINENTAL MKV OPEN CONVERTIBLE. BROOKLIN MODELS ISSUED THIS WHITE METAL REPLICA IN 1996. PART OF THE AUTHOR'S COLLECTION, IT RECEIVED CHROME AND GOLD DETAILING TO ITS BRIGHTWORK AT THE HANDS OF JIM HARDIN OF PROSCALE MODELS. MODEL NUMBER BRK-57. (AUTHOR COLLECTION)

Ford in miniature

1961 Lincoln Continental top up convertible by Bruce Arnold, number 2 of 3 for the Model Museum Collection. (Courtesy Bruce Arnold)

1965 Continental open convertible by Century Models of France. Crafted in white metal, this model came in four colors, including this light mint green. Model number 14. (Courtesy J Rettig)

Mini Marque '43' made these classic 1964 Continental models. The red sedan is model MMQ-26C. The only 4 door convertible since the 1940s, the Continental for 1964 was a desirable luxury motorcar. Mini Marque '43' model MMC-26B. (Courtesy A Thomas)

A sales success with 30,858 sold in its first year, Lincoln's 1969 Continental MkIII was an attractive personal luxury motorcar. The handbuilt white metal models pictured here come from Legendary Motorcars LLC; number 5 in a line that also includes replicas of General Motors' and Chrysler's luxury automobiles. Finished in maroon or metallic blue original colors with 'padded' tops. A stunning model of a beautiful car. The limited and numbered edition retails at $259. (Courtesy A Thomas)

Why not visit Veloce on the web? – WWW.VELOCEBOOKS.COM
New book news • Special offers • Details of all books in print • Gift vouchers

Mercury 4

A 1957 Mercury Turnpike Cruiser contingent: 2 door hard top coupé; convertible with white top up and continental wheel; pace car convertible with black top up and continental wheel. Mini Marque '43' model numbers MMQ-21A, 21B, and 21C. (Author collection)

Like rivals Pontiac and DeSoto, whose annual sales volumes historically ran in the middle of the pack, scale models (at least in 1:43) of Mercury cars have not been particularly plentiful. In fact, more variations of Lincolns have been produced than their lower-priced brethren.

Summary of major models

Only one Mercury model from the original years – 1939-1940 – was made; Brooklin Models' 1939 Mercury 99-A coupé. Brooklin has also produced a very nice Woody; the Sportsman from 1946. Brooklin also produced a replica of the 'bathtub' 1949 coupé model that attained near cult status in the classic James Dean movie, *Rebel without a cause*.

The '50s

Brooklin, Skyline (Germany), and Zaugg (Switzerland) made 1950 coupé and convertible models. Durham Classics (Canada) produced a substantial white metal 1951 Monarch that was a Canadian variation of the Mercury. Frobly of France also made a 1951 resin Mercury convertible.

Arguably the most detailed Mercury models produced were a range of 1955s from Motor City USA (USA), which made them initially under the Design Studio label and later as slightly less detailed USA Models. The Design Studio versions have details such as separate wipers and textured upholstery.

Argentine maker, Goldvarg Collection, issued one of its best proportioned and detailed models, the 1956 Montclair convertible.

1939 Mercury sedan coupé, issued by Brooklin Models in 2005. An extremely well-proportioned and faithful depiction of the original, this is the company's 117th standard model. (Courtesy D Mathyssen)

Ford in miniature

A 1959 Park Lane hardtop was pictured in the brochure but never produced.

The slightly bizarre 1957 Turnpike Cruiser (hardtop and convertible) was crafted by Brooklin and ABC Models (Italy), but perhaps the most accurate version came courtesy of Mini Marque '43' (UK).

Finally, Brooklin handmade the 1959 Commuter station wagon, an unusual choice which hobbyists who favor street versions cherish.

The 60s

FTA/Milestone Miniatures (UK) currently sells a 1966 Cyclone (hardtop and convertible). Zaugg made a 1968 Cyclone fastback, and Toys for Collectors (USA) released several 1968 Cougars.

Model-by-model 1939-1948

During the 1930s, Ford's senior management noticed a disturbing trend. As buyers became more affluent, they began to trade their V-8 Fords and Model As for brands such as Pontiac, Dodge, Nash, and even Packard. To stem the outflow of middle-income customers and ultimately provide a bridge to the Zephyr, Ford created the Mercury automobile.

This 'Big Ford' (a misnomer because it was actually very different to the smaller automobile) proved immediately popular and substantially augmented sales of the low-priced Ford throughout the 1940s.

For some reason, producers of scale models have tended to neglect the more common, mid-priced North American products of the 1930s and 1940s. Only Brooklin Models has seen fit to issue the 1939 Mercury 99-A coupé and 1946 Mercury Sportsman.

The only 1946 Mercury modeled in white metal is this well-proportioned and glossy Sportsman by Brooklin, number BRK-69. Brooklin does Woodies very well and they are well priced. (Courtesy D Mathyssen)

1946 Sportsman handmade in white metal in a light green for Modelex '98. Model number BRK-69. (Courtesy D Mathyssen)

1939 Mercury sedan coupé. John Roberts re-painted and detailed Brooklin's excellent version to create this one-off. Model number BRK-117. (Courtesy D Larsen)

MERCURY

Model-by-model — 1949-1951

As celebrated in the classic James Dean flick, *Rebel without a cause*, the Mercury models of 1949-1951 – the hot rodders' and customisers' favorite vehicle, and icon of 1950s style – were very popular, and more than 900,000 were sold in their three year run. Sharing a body with the entry level Lincoln helped differentiate the Mercury from the lower-priced Ford. In fact, it can be argued that at no other time did Mercury look more like a Lincoln and less like a Ford. Nonetheless, the strategy appeared to work as Ford Motor Company began to pull away from rivals at Highland Park with the somewhat stodgy, 'lookalike' range of Plymouths and Dodges.

Active modelers of 1:43 handbuilt replicas include Brooklin and Tin Wizard/Skyline. Defunct European makers Frobly and Zaugg also issued models for this time period, the masters of the latter being refined by Tin Wizard and used in the production of its Skyline range. Minichamps also makes a very nice die-cast model to commemorate Ford's Centennial.

In Canada, Lincoln-Mercury dealers had a lower-priced Mercury to sell as well, the Ford-based 'Meteor'. Many years ago, Jerry Rettig of Enchantment Land Coachbuilders, created a handbuilt 1:43 scale version of this car as a Mesquite Model.

1950 OPEN CONVERTIBLE BY SKYLINE MODELS. A VERY NICELY FINISHED MODEL. ORIGINALLY, ZAUGG MADE THIS MODEL BUT EVENTUALLY TIN WIZARD, A GERMAN BUILDER WHICH PRODUCES MANY FINE MODELS, ACQUIRED THE ZAUGG CASTINGS. SKYLINE MODELS IS TIN WIZARD'S AMERICAN MODELS LINE. THIS IS NUMBER 503. (COURTESY TIN WIZARD)

ANOTHER VIEW OF THE 1950 MERCURY CONVERTIBLE. ONLY FIVE PER CENT OF MERCURY AUTOMOBILES PRODUCED IN 1950 WERE CONVERTIBLES. SKYLINE MODELS NUMBER 503. (COURTESY TIN WIZARD)

1950 2 DOOR COUPÉ BY SKYLINE MODELS. THIS FIRE CHIEF'S CAR FEATURES CORRECT FDNY SIGNAGE AND DOOR INSIGNIA. MODEL NUMBER 502. (COURTESY TIN WIZARD)

1950 MERCURY CLUB COUPÉ BY ZAUGG MODELS OF SWITZERLAND. LACK OF DETAILS LIKE WINDSHIELD WIPERS, SEPARATE DOOR HANDLES AND OTHER BRIGHTWORK GIVE EVIDENCE THAT THIS RESIN MODEL WAS PRODUCED BEFORE THE MID-1980S. NOTICE, HOWEVER, THE GOOD PROPORTIONS AND ACCURATE SCULPTING OF THE BODY. CARE WAS GIVEN TO THE QUITE ORNATE HOOD MASCOT THAT REALLY SETS OFF THE APPEARANCE OF THE CAR AND DISTINGUISHES IT FROM CHEAPER DIE-CAST SCALE MODELS. THIS IS MODEL NUMBER 5. (COURTESY J RETTIG)

RIGHT: 1950 2 DOOR COUPÉ BY SKYLINE MODELS IN A GREEN-HUED CIVILIAN VERSION, NUMBER 501. (COURTESY TOYS FOR COLLECTORS USA)

Ford in miniature

Brooklin Models' 1949 coupé was such a roaring success that the builder issued a follow-up model in 1994 – this slightly more detailed 1950 Mercury open convertible, model number BRK-15a. (Courtesy D Mathyssen)

1949 Mercury 2 door sedan, Brooklin Models number 15. The standard issue model was cream and then green, and went to a few thousand collectors. The dark metallic blue with red interior number shown here is one of 200 produced for Miniature Cars in 1991. A very substantial, white metal example that weighs in at close to a pound, the model has precise proportions and accurate moldings (note the authentic-looking grille texture). As with most early Brooklin models, this Merc is a little plain with brightwork confined to grille and bumpers. (Courtesy D Mathyssen)

A detailed version with plenty of chrome foil added. 1949 Mercury 2 door sedan by Brooklin, number 15. (Courtesy D Larsen)

Left: 1949 Mercury 2 door sedan. This black number with Omen figure of James Dean was issued for Brooklin Club Deutschland in 1992; it is 1 of 200. (Courtesy D Mathyssen)

Above: A strikingly attractive replica is this 1950 Mercury top down convertible with wire wheels handcrafted by Dean Paolucci of DMP Studios, the nicest 1950 Brooklin Mercury I have ever seen. Only 50 of these Code 2 replicas went to lucky collectors. DMP Studios. (Photo Don Markle; model courtesy D Paolucci)

MERCURY

ANOTHER VIEW OF DEAN PAOLUCCI'S 1950 BROOKLIN MERCURY WHICH SHOWS THE MODELER HAS PICKED OUT INTERIOR DETAILS SUCH AS THE WINDOW WINDERS IN SILVER. NOTE ALSO THE CANVAS EFFECT ON THE CONVERTIBLE BOOT COVER. DMP STUDIOS. (PHOTO DON MARKLE; MODEL COURTESY D PAOLUCCI)

1950 INDIANAPOLIS 500 PACE CAR BY SKYLINE MODELS. MODEL NUMBER 504. (COURTESY TIN WIZARD)

FROBLY OF FRANCE ISSUED THIS HANDBUILT 1951 MERCURY CONVERTIBLE IN WHITE METAL. PICTURED IS THE LESS COMMON TOP UP MODEL IN AN ATTRACTIVE GREEN WITH CREAM TOP. SCALING OUT AT 1:44, FROBLY'S LEVEL OF DETAILING IS MIDWAY BETWEEN BROOKLIN'S MERCURY AND THE SKYLINE/TIN WIZARD, ALTHOUGH THIS MODEL FROM JERRY RETTIG APPEARS TO HAVE RECEIVED EXTRA ATTENTION WITH CHROME FOIL ALONG THE SIDE, AT THE TOP OF THE DOORS, AND AROUND THE WINDSHIELD, MAKING IT A VERY ATTRACTIVE REPLICA. MODEL NUMBER 2A. (COURTESY J RETTIG)

Model-by-model 1952-1956

With the exception of the 1956 Lincoln, a strong family resemblance existed across the three Ford Motor Company lines for model years 1952-1956. These were lukewarm sales years for Mercury as it struggled to maintain market share in the crowded mid-price range.

Few handbuilt model cars from this five-year period representing Mercury automobiles exist. Motor City USA released a few versions during the 1990-2004 period, a superb 1955 hardtop coupé, and convertible, and Sun Valley. Argentine builder, Goldvarg, sold a 1956 convertible. Collectors' Classics, also of Argentina, issued a few thousand nice 1954 die-cast replicas.

CONTINUED PAGE 99

1954 SUN VALLEY IN GREEN, AND MONTEREY TOP UP CONVERTIBLE IN WHITE. COLLECTORS' CLASSICS DIE-CAST MODELS. (AUTHOR COLLECTION)

Ford in Miniature

1954 Monterey top up convertible in white. A Collectors' Classics die-cast model. Model number 3U. (Author collection)

This navy 1955 Montclair convertible is from Motor City USA, an interim model between the builder's high-level Design Studios line and its most recent American Models line. It was a well-detailed model which retailed at around $125 and was comparable to Western Models offerings. USA-24. (Author collection)

1954 Mercury Sun Valley hard top, model 3H by Collectors' Classics of Argentina. (Author collection)

1954 Monterey top up convertible in Roman Red from Collectors' Classics. Model 3U. (Author collection)

In the author's opinion, the most detailed and nicely-finished Mercury models issued in 1:43 scale white metal are those from Motor City USA's early Design Studio Line. Linger over the photographs of the 1955 Mercury models on the next few pages and you will see what I mean. Left to right: Sun Valley (number DS-10); Montclair convertible (number DS-10C); Montclair 2 door hard top coupé (number DS-10H). (Author collection)

A pair of 1954 Mercury convertibles (number 3U) in top up mode which show the attractive genuine Mercury colors. Also available were two shades of green, two shades of metallic blue, and a light yellow. Collectors' Classics also offered these models as an open version (number 3D). (Author collection)

1955 Sun Valley, Design Studio handbuilt model number DS-10 made from white metal. It is perfectly proportioned, finished, and detailed down to the logos on each wheel cover. Expect to pay upwards of $200 – if you can find one. (Author collection)

1955 SUN VALLEY WITH CONTINENTAL WHEEL BY DESIGN STUDIO, MODEL NUMBER DS-10. MOTOR CITY USA FINISHED ITS MODELS IN AUTHENTIC MERCURY COLORS, LIKE THIS LUSTROUS YUKON YELLOW WITH BLACK. (AUTHOR COLLECTION)

1955 MONTCLAIR TOP DOWN CONVERTIBLE IN CANYON CORDOVAN FROM DESIGN STUDIO, MODEL NUMBER DS-10C. (AUTHOR COLLECTION)

1955 MONTCLAIR OPEN CONVERTIBLE WITH CONTINENTAL KIT. THE DEGREE OF DETAIL ON THIS MODEL IS PHENOMENAL. DESIGN STUDIOS MODEL NUMBER 10C. (AUTHOR COLLECTION)

A BIRD'S-EYE VIEW OF THE PRINTED INTERIOR OF DESIGN STUDIO'S '55 MERCURY. THE HARD TOP AND CONVERTIBLE MODELS WERE REISSUED WITH SLIGHTLY LESS DETAIL IN 2004 AS PART OF MOTOR CITY USA'S AMERICAN MODELS LINE, BUT WITHOUT THE UNIQUE SEAT PATTERN OF THIS MODEL. (AUTHOR COLLECTION)

1955 MONTCLAIR 2 DOOR HARD TOP COUPÉ FROM DESIGN STUDIOS, NUMBER DS-10H. A BEAUTIFUL MODEL HANDMADE IN 1:43 SCALE FROM WHITE METAL. UNLIKE ITS MANY COMPETITORS, MERCURY'S USE OF MULTI-TONED COLORS WAS QUITE RESTRAINED. HERE, IN ADDITION TO THE GREEN BODY AND WHITE ROOF, MERCURY ADDED ATTRACTIVE CONTRASTING RED WHEEL TRIM RINGS, AN INEXPENSIVE BUT EFFECTIVE USE OF COLOR. (AUTHOR COLLECTION)

BELOW: 1955 MONTCLAIR 2 DOOR HARD TOP COUPÉ. THE COLOR OF THIS MODEL IS ARBOUR GREEN. THE BUILDER MAKES EXTENSIVE USE OF CHROME FOIL, AND SMALL EMBLEM PIECES ARE NICKEL-PLATED WHITE METAL. ONLY FOR THE EXTREMELY SMALL LETTERING IN THE MERCURY SCRIPT ON THE HOOD HAS THE BUILDER RESORTED TO THE USE OF A DECAL. TO USE PHOTO-ETCHED MATERIALS FOR DETAIL THIS SMALL WOULD ADD PROHIBITIVELY TO THE COMPLEXITY AND PRICE OF THE MODEL. DESIGN STUDIOS MODEL NUMBER 10H. (AUTHOR COLLECTION)

Ford in miniature

Unlike the convertible and Sun Valley models, the builder has not added a continental wheel to the 1955 Mercury hard top, which allows the intricate rear emblem to be seen. Model number DS-10H. (Author collection)

1956 Montclair top down convertible from Goldvarg. This ivory and turquoise convertible is a 1956 model, number 7. Goldvarg models were noted for their very solid construction; this example also has quite a bit of detail. (Courtesy J Rettig)

Model-by-model   1957-1959

1955 Sun Valley, open convertible and hard top. Note the release handle on the right of each continental wheel. Design Studio model numbers 10, 10-C and 10H. (Author collection)

Some consider that the redesigned 1955 Mercury looks more massive than the more senior Lincoln of the same year; here are both models for comparison. The Lincoln Capri is Motor City USA model number MC-65; the Mercury Sun Valley is Design Studio model number DS-10. The elevated view shows the tinted Plexiglas roof insert of the Sun Valley offering. Mercury produced 1787 Sun Valley models that year; sales of Design Studio and American Models replicas was about half that figure. (Author collection)

Mercury's 1957 Turnpike Cruiser was Ford Motor Company's entry in that year's 'excess derby'. Equipment that just a few years before would have been found on experimental vehicles only appeared on Mercury's flagship model. Twin horizontal radio antennae, 'Breezeway' rear window, keyboard Merc-O-Matic, Seat-o-Matic, and many other appearance and electric gizmos were used to compete in the crowded, medium price market sector. The three Mini Marque '43' models in this photograph are, clockwise from top: top up convertible pace car with continental wheel, number MMQ-21C; top up convertible, number MMQ-21B; 2 door hard top, number MMQ-21A. (Author collection)

MERCURY

Historians – and even designers – view the last few years of the 1950s as a time of rampant excess when it came to motorcar styling. Cars from this era were often huge, with chrome draped over both interior and exterior surfaces. Clearly, it was not a time of restraint and Mercury models fit right in with the times.

Mercury added a number of styling innovations to existing ideas such as a horizontal radio antennae protruding from the windshield frame, and the reverse canted 'Breezeway' rear window. The former disappeared with the 1957 model year whilst the latter was adopted by the senior Lincolns and became a Mercury styling signature until 1967.

As for replicas of this benighted period, eccentric and passionate producer, Richard Briggs, issued a few hundred 1957 Turnpike hardtops and convertibles in his Mini Marque '43' line-up. The pace car is the most common and comes up frequently in auctions. Brooklin Models' 1959 Commuter station wagon is an intriguing white metal model still available from retailers.

A FRONT VIEW OF THREE 1957 TURNPIKE MODELS IN THE MMQ-21 SERIES. MINI MARQUE '43' MODELED SOME FINE 1957-59 FORD PRODUCTS, INCLUDING FORD, EDSEL, AND LINCOLN. MANY WERE AVAILABLE WITH A CONTINENTAL WHEEL. THE REAR FENDERS OF THE TURNPIKE HAD A HIGHLY REFLECTIVE METALLIC INSERT THAT CATCHES THE COLORS OF ITS SURROUNDINGS, IN THIS CASE MAKING IT APPEAR RED. (AUTHOR COLLECTION)

1957 TURNPIKE CRUISER 2 DOOR HARD TOP. THIS MINI MARQUE '43' HANDBUILT WHITE METAL MODEL HAS SOME SUBTLE TOUCHES – SUCH AS SIDE WINDOWS IN THE UP POSITION AND THE CHROME DIVIDE BETWEEN FRONT AND REAR WINDOWS – WHICH ENHANCE ITS ACCURACY AND JUSTIFY THE MODEL'S ORIGINAL PRICE OF $200. (COURTESY D LARSEN)

1957 TURNPIKE CRUISER TOP UP CONVERTIBLE PACE CAR. MERCURY PRODUCED FOUR OFFICIAL PACE CARS FOR THE INDIANAPOLIS 500. THE DIVISION ALSO MADE SEVERAL OTHER TURNPIKE CONVERTIBLES WITH PACE CAR DECALS FOR DEALERS TO DISPLAY. MINI MARQUE '43' MODEL NUMBER 21C. (AUTHOR COLLECTION)

THIS PHOTO ILLUSTRATES HOW THE ADDITION OF A BUMPER-MOUNTED CONTINENTAL WHEEL ADDED ANOTHER FOOT-AND-A-HALF TO AN ALREADY LONG, 211 INCH MOTORCAR. 1957 TURNPIKE CRUISER CONVERTIBLE AND 2 DOOR HARD TOP BY MINI MARQUE '43'. (AUTHOR COLLECTION)

Ford in miniature

1957 Turnpike Cruiser top up convertible pace car. Mini Marque '43' model number 21C. (Author collection)

The builder successfully captured the distinctive futuristic dashboard and instrument panel design of the Turnpike Cruiser. (Author collection)

1957 Turnpike Cruiser convertible pace car atop an early Mini Marque '43' box. Despite its high build quality and level of detail, this replica has not tended to maintain value, at least as at the time of publication. This is quite unusual and may be due to the greater than usual number issued by the builder. (Author collection)

Brooklin also issued a metallic copper version of the 1957 Turnpike Cruiser, numbered BRK-28, in 1988. It is a lightly detailed model. (Courtesy D Mathyssen)

A surprising 1959 Mercury commuter station wagon in Canton Red and white from Brooklin. This model, number BRK-77, is one of the few late '50s wagons modeled by any builder. It has a bubble-type windshield and 'Quadra-Beam' headlights. (Courtesy D Mathyssen)

Below: A further 200 light green and white 1959 Mercury commuter station wagon models were released by Brooklin for the 1999 Modelex Show. (Courtesy D Mathyssen)

MERCURY

Model-by-model   1960-1969

Within its market segment of mid-priced offerings, Mercury held its own during the 1960s. Within the Ford Motor Company it kept pace with the Ford Division through introduction of the Comet and Cougar, both higher priced versions of the Fairlane/Torino and Mustang.

Scale models of Mercurys from 1960-69 are few and far between, especially if sought in 1:43rd scale. The number of models can be counted on the fingers of one hand: in handbuilt white metal, 1966 Comet and 1967 Cougar from Milestone Miniatures and Toys for Collectors; 1968 Cyclone GT from Zaugg. In die-cast, a somewhat plain but very inexpensive Yat Ming 1964 Montclair 2 door hardtop, and, finally, a well proportioned and detailed 1969 Marauder fastback from Minichamps.

FRONT AND REAR VIEWS OF A 1968 CYCLONE GT FASTBACK FROM ZAUGG. PATTERN BASED ON AMT FORD TORINO. THIS SELDOM SEEN MODEL HAS SOME NICE DETAILS SUCH AS MAG-INSPIRED CHROME WHEELS. MODEL NUMBER 140. (PHOTO COURTESY J M ARNOLD; MODEL COURTESY B ARNOLD)

MID-1960 MERCURYS HAVE NOT BEEN A POPULAR SUBJECT WITH HANDMADE MODEL BUILDERS. YATMING RECENTLY RELEASED THIS NICE 1964 MAURAUDER IN THE RIDICULOUSLY LOW PRICE RANGE OF $5-10. ADVERTISED AS 'HANDMADE', IT CANNOT MATCH THE QUALITY, FEEL, NOR EXCLUSIVITY OF A HANDBUILT RESIN OR WHITE METAL MODEL, BUT IS A GOOD 'GAP FILLER' FOR A COLLECTION, AND SHOWS HOW FAR THE MANUFACTURING PROCESS HAS ADVANCED IN A FEW DECADES. (AUTHOR COLLECTION)

FRONT AND REAR VIEWS OF A 1969 COUGAR XR-7 HARD TOP COUPÉ FROM AMT, A POLYSTYRENE 1:43 SCALE MODEL BUILT AND DETAILED BY BRUCE ARNOLD. (PHOTO COURTESY J M ARNOLD; MODEL COURTESY B ARNOLD)

Ford in miniature

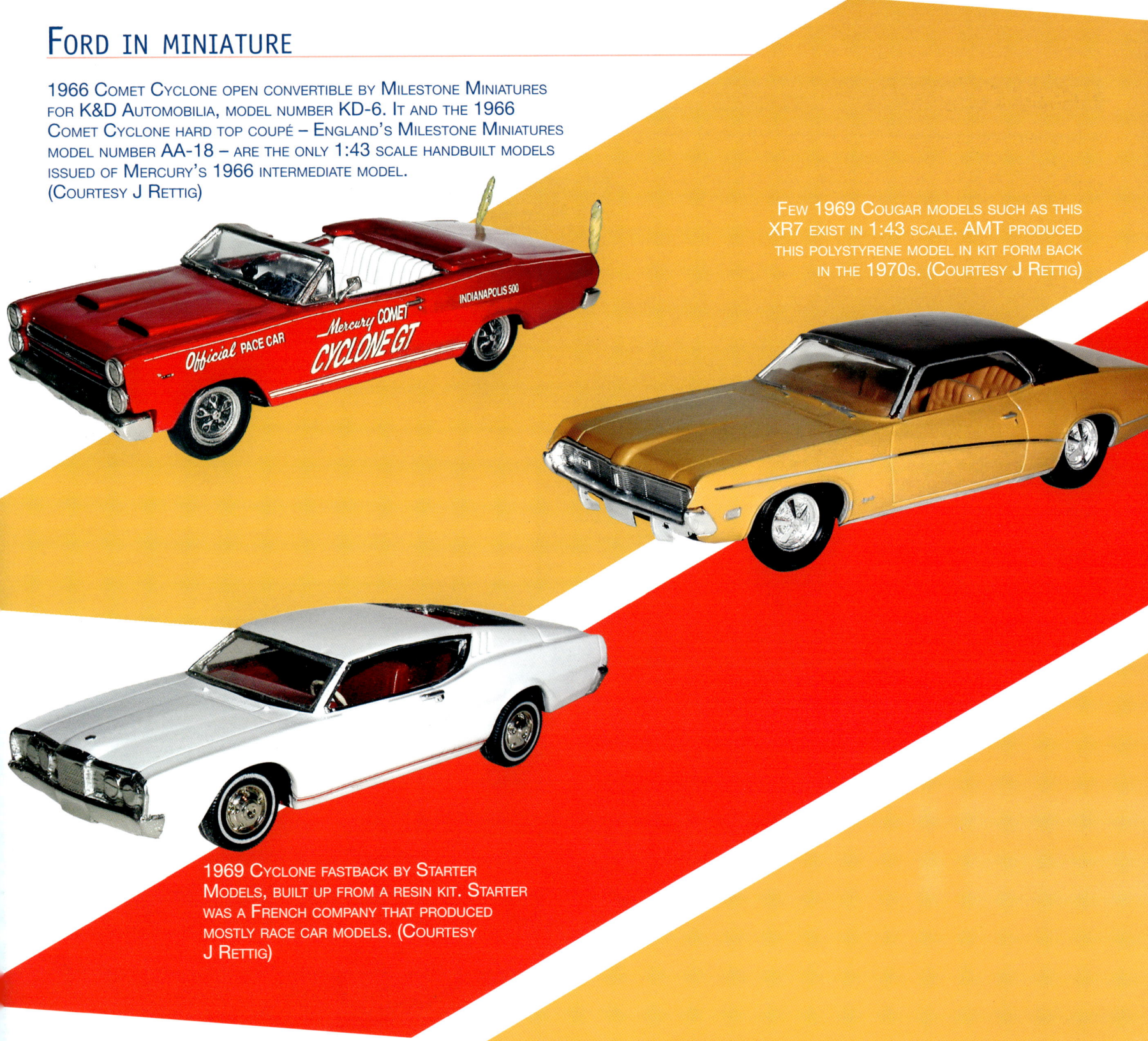

1966 Comet Cyclone open convertible by Milestone Miniatures for K&D Automobilia, model number KD-6. It and the 1966 Comet Cyclone hard top coupé – England's Milestone Miniatures model number AA-18 – are the only 1:43 scale handbuilt models issued of Mercury's 1966 intermediate model. (Courtesy J Rettig)

Few 1969 Cougar models such as this XR7 exist in 1:43 scale. AMT produced this polystyrene model in kit form back in the 1970s. (Courtesy J Rettig)

1969 Cyclone fastback by Starter Models, built up from a resin kit. Starter was a French company that produced mostly race car models. (Courtesy J Rettig)

Why not visit Veloce on the web? – www.velocebooks.com
New book news • Special offers • Details of all books in print • Gift vouchers

BUILDERS 5

I STRUGGLED A LITTLE BIT WITH THE TITLE OF this chapter: what, after all, constitutes a builder?

There exist a few gifted sculptors capable of creating wonderful works of art using their eyes, mind, and hands. Others deftly take the parts these people fashion and assemble them carefully and with uncanny precision. There are people who invent and refine processes and tools to make the product more detailed, durable and realistic in substance and appearance. Still others commission a model to be built and enable it to be by breathing life and resources into it. There are those who assemble and manage the production team. Others take an existing design and create something from it that becomes an entirely new model of its own.

Not all of those who create handbuilt model cars actually build them personally, yet, in their own way, all of the people I have just described are builders. Through their vision and action they have enabled these wondrous models to be.

1957 FORD DEL RIO STATION WAGON BY MINI MARQUE '43' AND 1939 FORD DELUXE STATION WAGON, AMERICAN MODELS LINE OF MOTOR CITY USA. MODEL NUMBERS MMQ-19 AND AM-1. (AUTHOR COLLECTION)

This chapter recognizes many of the people who are responsible for building the models of Ford Motor Company products featured in this book. Some of the companies I describe are no longer active; still others have changed hands. I have omitted some builders because of a lack of available information about them. The remainder – such as the very fine Bruce Arnold Models, Great American Dream Machines, Midlantic Models, Victory models, Shrock Brothers, and others – have not been included because the models they produce are outside the scope of this book. (I hope to cover their models in a separate volume.)

On a final note, I would appreciate receiving – via my publisher – any information readers are willing to provide me with about defunct companies I have or have not listed.

1958 FORD THUNDERBIRD OPEN CONVERTIBLE. A&S MODELMAKERS NUMBER 1. (AUTHOR COLLECTION)

Ford in Miniature

A&S Modelmakers

A&S Modelmakers very much fits the description of a family-run artisan business. Alastair and Sally Duncan, who were based in Lincolnshire, England, were a husband-and-wife team which collaborated to build some beautiful models. Alastair built the patterns and together they painted and assembled the models.

During the late 1980s to early 1990s period, A&S issued two different models; a 1958 Thunderbird and 1958 Oldsmobile 98, each as a convertible and 2 door hardtop coupé. They are worthy of mention because of their exceptionally fine proportions, variety of colors, superb detailing – including full interiors with window winders and door handles – and overall superior quality. Despite cellophane windows that cloud a bit over time, these are a real treat to have as part of a collection.

When A&S ceased production around 1995, its patterns were sold to Mini Marque '43'. This company continued to issue the Thunderbird.

Ashton Models

A 1936 Ford long wheelbase sedan from Ashton Models. Handbuilt in white metal, this is model number 10. (Courtesy D Larsen)

Founded by Gerhard Klarwasser in 1983, Ashton Models is a Czech builder of superb models; primarily fire trucks and related apparatus. Limited usually to 100-250 pieces, the builder's models are handbuilt in 1:43 scale. Although Ashton Models now sells truck models exclusively through a small number of suppliers, its first seven models included a 1961 Thunderbird, 1936 Ford long wheelbase sedan, 1953 Ford F-100 pickup, and 1957 Ford 4 door sedan in civilian and fire chief liveries. Bruce Arnold informs me that the latter, which is quite a crude model, is a "white metal copy of an ancient Schucco 1957 Ford 4 door sedan". All models are rare today.

Auto Buff

One of the first builders to market fully built-up models, this California, USA company, initially called Le Buff Stuff, was started by Barry Lester, an early scratch builder and white metal casting pioneer. His line was entirely devoted to the Ford product.

Unavailable at hobby stores but occasionally seen at auctions, garage sales and flea markets, the models may seem a little unrefined and, on occasion, not of the stated 1:43rd scale. Sometimes an amateur hobbyist built the models one sees today. Built-up models from Auto Buff are better finished. Look past all of this, however, and you can enjoy the model for what it is; an artistic effort to capture a piece of automotive history by capable craftspeople.

Models include: 1928 roadsters, pickups and coupés; 1936 coupé, roadster, and 2 door sedan; 1940 coupé, 2 door sedan, convertible, and stake truck; 1948 club coupé and convertible; 1949 Ford Tudor sedan; 1953 pickup, panel, and stake truck.

BBR

BBR usually models European motorcars. However, it carefully crafted the 1952 Lincoln number 17A pictured below. BBR also made 1953 and 1954 model years, numbers 17E & 17L. According to expert, Bruce Arnold (who has seen all models): "The builders have sometimes confused years, resulting in a curious mix of trim. Those collectors used to white metal models may find these delicate". Exquisitely crafted and presented in resin, the market price of these models is around $300. Under the Styling Models Line, BBR still lists as available (at time of printing) the models in the accompanying table opposite.

Lincoln 1952 Capri V 8 coupé. BBR Models number 17A. (Courtesy D Larsen)

Belgium Trucks/Jupiter

This company from Belgium, of course, issued a 1960 Thunderbird supplied by A&S Modelmakers (see foregoing). Says Bruce Arnold: "Sadly, the 1960 Thunderbird by Belgium Trucks was

BUILDERS

BBR Styling Models line

LINCOLN 1952 SM17A CAPRI V 8 COUPÉ
LINCOLN 1952 SM17O CAPRI V 8 COUPÉ-MANTZ
LINCOLN 1952 SM17P CAPRI V 8 COUPÉ-STEVENSON
LINCOLN 1953 SM17E CAPRI V 8 COUPÉ
LINCOLN 1953 SM17Q CAPRI V 8 COUPÉ-STEVENSON
LINCOLN 1954 SM17L CAPRI V 8 COUPÉ
LINCOLN 1954 SM17R CAPRI V 8 COUPÉ-CRAWFORD

very poorly proportioned. The later A&S 1958 Thunderbird had the many flaws corrected. The real gem from Jupiter, however, is Peter Kenna's 1960 Plymouth Valiant, modeled in both wagon and sedan forms. This is a must for any serious collector".

Brooklin Models

BROOKLIN MODELS BOX AND ANNUAL CATALOGUE OF MODELS FROM AUTHOR'S COLLECTION. (AUTHOR COLLECTION)

Like many collectors of handbuilts, my first model was a Brooklin. It turned out to be the company's first ever model; the 1933 Pierce Arrow sedan, produced during Brooklin's early days in Canada. Brooklin is the largest builder of handbuilt models which often produces more than a thousand models in each number and has a worldwide following with model clubs in several countries. Hefty weight, excellent paint finish and assembly, a wide assortment of available models, and attractive pricing below $100 characterize Brooklin models. Initially on some early models, proportions and detail were lacking somewhat, though the models had a charm, almost like an impression of the real model rather than an exact smaller-sized copy. At this point, new models have more detail, are well-proportioned, and represent excellent value.

Bruce Arnold again: "Brooklin patternmaker, Ian Pickering, is clearly the best in the world. He makes most of his American car patterns from photographs alone. Challenged in the 1990s by more accurate competitors, Brooklin stepped up to the plate in a most formidable way, satisfyig even the most ardent ccritics. Virtually every new release is a masterpiece".

Comment from Dick Browne, Brooklin authority
It's Brooklin not Brooklyn!
"I can understand the confusion but the first home of Brooklin Models was the Canadian village of Brooklin, Ontario, hence the name. In 1974 John Hall, gave up his previous careers as a design engineer and a college teacher to devote his full time efforts to producing 1:43 scale model cars. From the beginning Brooklin Models specialized in models of cars not generally produced by other manufacturers. The very first Brooklin was the 1933 Pierce Silver Arrow Sedan, followed by a Tucker Torpedo and a Ford Model A Victoria.

"In 1979 John and his wife Jenny decided to move their family back to England where they had been born and raised. They decided on the lovely city of Bath in south west England and that is where Brooklin Models Ltd continues in business today. In 1998 John and Jenny decided to retire and Nigel Parker and a team of other Brooklin employees bought the company. Brooklin Models continues as the largest manufacturer of handbuilt white metal models in the world.

"As of the end of 2006, over 120 different American cars, light trucks and trailers, in over 600 varieties, have been created for the Brooklin Collection, representing American cars and light trucks of the 1930s, '40s, '50s, and '60s. In addition, British cars are made in the Lansdowne line and Swedish cars in the Rob Eddie line. Recently, lines of International Police Vehicles, Community Service Vehicles, and Hot Rods have been produced. For 2005, Community Service Vehicles will also join the collections. In addition, US Model Mint trucks and trailers are also produced by Brooklin Models Ltd.

"Brooklin may be the only manufacturer to be supported by three different active clubs. There is the San Francisco Bay Brooklin Club in the US, and the Brooklin Collectors' Club and the Lansdowne Collectors' Club in the UK. All three groups have active programs including newsletters and annual model specials. Brooklin Models is also actively supported in Canada by the Canadian Toy Collectors' Society, of which John Hall was one of the founders, and by the Wessex Model & Toy Collectors

Ford in Miniature

Ford Motor Company models from Brooklin

Number	Year	Marque/model	Comments
BRK 3	1930	Ford Victoria	
BRK 5	1930	Ford Model A 2dr Sedan	
BRK 9	1940	Ford Sedan Delivery	Several versions
BRK 11	1956	Lincoln Continental MkII	
BRK 13	1956	Ford Thunderbird hardtop	Also sold with 1955 as set number 13X
BRK 13A	1957	Ford Thunderbird convertible – Open	
BRK 15	1949	Mercury 2 dr sedan	
BRK 15X	1949	Monarch coupé	CTCS
BRK 22	1958	Edsel Citation	Number 22A has continental wheel
BRK 23	1956	Ford Fairlane 2dr hardtop	
BRK 23AA	1956	Ford Mainline	
BRK 24	1968	Mustang Shelby fastback	Number 24A is a non-Shelby version
BRK 28	1957	Mercury Turnpike Cruiser	Number 28P is a convertible top-down pace car
BRK 28X	1957	Monarch 2dr hardtop	CTCS 1988, 1 of 450
BRK 35	1957	Ford Skyliner convertible	
BRK 37	1960	Ford Sunliner convertible	
BRK 42B	1952	Ford Ranger	
BRK 47	1965	Ford Thunderbird convertible – Open	
BRK 51	1951	Ford Victoria 2dr hardtop	
BRK 51A	1951	Ford 4dr sedan	Police car and Taxi for CTCS
BRK 51A	1951	Ford 4dr sedan	Police car and Taxi for CTCS
BRK 56	1965	Ford Mustang convertible	Pace car number 56P
BRK 57	1960	Lincoln Continental MkV convertible	
BRK 58	1963	Ford Falcon Sprint	
BRK 64	1959	Ford Thunderbird	
BRK 64A	1959	Ford Thunderbird	
BRK 69	1946	Mercury Sportsman Woody convertible	
BRK 75	1960	Edsel Ranger convertible	
BRK 76	1948	Ford F1 pickup	
BRK 77	1959	Mercury Commuter station wagon	
BRK 83	1947	Ford V8 station wagon	
BRK 92	1967	Ford Thunderbird 4dr landau	
BRK 94	1949	Lincoln Cosmopolitan convertible - top down	
BRK 94A	1949	Lincoln Cosmopolitan convertible	
BRK 99	1956	Lincoln Premier	
BRK 106	1938	Lincoln Zephyr 4dr sedan	
BRK 108	1957	Ford Ranchero pickup	
BRK 112	1963	Ford Falcon convertible	
BRK 117	1939	Mercury sedan 99-A coupé	

in England. These two clubs also have annual model specials.

"Through my associations with the clubs in the US and England I have enjoyed many warm friendships that have come to be even more important than the models. I have been privileged to get to know the people at Brooklin Models Ltd, and been called upon for assistance in getting them information. Recently, I was able to contribute further by measuring and photographing a rare car that was produced in 2004 as a model. It has been a great relationship. I shall look forward to many more years of collecting Brooklins."

Collectors' Classics

In the 1980s, Carlos Buby, a children's toy manufacturer in

BUILDERS

Argentina, produced a line of affordable collectors' automobile models. Appropriately called Collectors' Classics, these models were die-cast but hand assembled, with each model having a tag hand-signed by its assembler. The models featured a moderate level of detail, authentic manufacturer's colors, and were well-priced in the $30 range. According to Bruce Arnold: "The cost of employing and training so many people to assemble the complicated models" was a drain on the Buby enterprise. After Collectors' Classics "Buby never made another model".

Despite large issue numbers – usually around 20,000 pieces– Collectors' Classics models have retained their popularity and have, in some instances, most notably the 1953 Ford and 1954 Mercury versions, even increased in price amongst collectors.

Aside from being slightly over-wide, the Collectors' Classics replicas would do any Ford model collection proud.

well-detailed, making extensive use of photo etching. They will stand up against any other handbuilt model in their faithfulness to the original car upon which they are modeled. If you can get one, expect to pay in the high $100s to $300.

"Henk van Asten" says Bruce Arnold "was a man with a mission. There was no money to be made in the virtually non-existent, high quality, hand-built 1:43 market in the 1980s. As he progressed, thankfully, he got away from an early tendency to make Conquest/Madison models wider than scale – a practice he defended by claiming that some subjects do not look imposing enough when scaled down to 1:43. By the time my 1947 Studebaker Champion (Madison model number 19) amd 1947 Cadillac Fleetwood 75 limousine (Conquest model number 30) were produced, accuracy and scale fidelity of Fa. Daimler House models were brought more into focus".

1954 MERCURY TOP UP FROM COLLECTORS' CLASSICS WITH ORIGINAL BOX. NOTE THE CERTIFICATE STAMPED WITH PIECE NUMBER '9021', WHICH PROVIDES AN INDICATION OF THE LARGE PRODUCTION VOLUMES THAT DIE-CAST MODELS ENJOY. THE MAKER'S BOX IS ALSO DECORATED WITH THE LOGOS OF FAMOUS AUTOMOBILE MARQUES. A FEW MODEL COMPANIES, NOTABLY SUN AND OAKLAND, FEATURED PHOTOGRAPHS OF MODELS ON THEIR BOXES. TODAY, THIS IS RARELY DONE. ALTHOUGH MANUFACTURERS OF HANDBUILTS USUALLY STRIVE TO PROVIDE DISTINCTIVE PACKAGING, IN ITSELF IT RARELY COMMANDS HIGH PRICES AS IT DOES WITH DINKY TOYS AND CORGI TOYS PACKAGING. (AUTHOR COLLECTION)

1957 THUNDERBIRD WITH BOX, BOOKLETS AND PEN FROM FA. DAIMLER HOUSE/ CONQUEST MODELS. HENK VAN ASTEN INCLUDED A CATALOGUE OF MODELS WITH EVERY REPLICA THAT FA. DAIMLER HOUSE SOLD. SEVEN EDITIONS OF THE FULL COLOR CATALOGUE WERE PRODUCED AND EACH IS A FASCINATING RECORD OF THE MODELS THIS PRESTIGIOUS MAKER ISSUED. AS A SOUVENIR, NEW CONQUEST OWNER, BUZ KIRKEL, PROVIDES PURCHASERS WITH A CONQUEST BALLPOINT PEN. (AUTHOR COLLECTION)

CONQUEST MADISON

Conquest and Madison Models are now owned by Dave 'Buz' Kirkel of Route 66 Model Car Store.

Between 1987 and 2003, beautiful and interesting models were released by Henk van Asten's Fa. Daimler House in Holland.

Henk commissioned the SMTS factory to produce a range of replicas of models from the late '40s to the early '60s, often in sedan and station wagon body styles. Conquest, Madison, and Light Duty Models are accurately finished, well-proportioned, and

Henk van Asten says: "Being born in 1946, I got my first Dinky Toys models in 1956; one each month. Finally, I had about 20 models to play with. A few of these Dinky models have survived, badly worn, alas. Later, I became a teacher at a high school in economic science and trade science (book-keeping etc).

"One day in 1972, on my way home from school, I 'discovered' a shop in a village which still had many old Dinkies from the sixties. I bought about 20 or 25 of these, and that was the start of my collection. Real collecting began about four years later. Of course, the Dinky range is a limited one, so I also started to collect Corgi, Spot-On and other makes in 1:43rd scale, and visited swap meets. I also began to trade in these models.

"To enlarge my collection, I also started to add handbuilt models. Still, a lot of models of the real cars were not available. Then, I thought, why not release these myself?

"Preparation to launch my own ranges started in 1983. Because a lot of detailing can be done on American cars (contrary

Ford in Miniature

to the 'plain' British and European cars), I chose to release nice American car models.

"After some time, I found in SMTS, a company which could supply me with the models in a quality I wanted, and released the first Madison in 1987. The first Conquest followed about four months later in October 1987. To sell these, I founded Fa. Daimler House. Sales quickly increased and I stopped teaching. I released many models in the 1987-2002 time period. Since 2002, I only make re-runs (made by SMTS) of my models, depending on demand.

"From 1973 to 2003, I also owned one or more classic cars, always British ones (Rover, Bentley, Daimler); in fact mainly Daimlers. I had a Daimler Conquest from 1974 to about 1992. Hence, I named my company Fa. Daimler House, and one range I named Conquest Models. 'Madison' is a fantasy name, which sounds American."

DURHAM CLASSICS AUTOMOTIVE MINIATURES PROVIDED A DISTINCTIVE SILVER OR GOLD FOILED BOX AND A SIGNED CERTIFICATE STATING THE NUMBER OF MODELS ISSUED. THE FORD COURIER HERE IN AVRO AIRCRAFT COLORS WAS ONE OF 350 TOTAL HANDMADE PIECES. (AUTHOR COLLECTION)

Ford Motor Company models from Conquest Madison

Number	Year	Marque/model	Comments
CNQ-4	1963	Ford Galaxie 500 hardtop and convertible	1990 release
CNQ-9	1963	Ford Country Squire Woody station wagon	1991 release
CNQ-10	1950	Lincoln Cosmopolitan 4dr sedan	1992 release
CNQ-16	1957	Ford Thunderbird	1993 release, Porthole hardtop
CNQ-28	1957	Ford Thunderbird Roadster	1997 release, top down
MAD-2	1956	Lincoln Premier 4dr sedan	1988
MAD-5	1956	Lincoln Premiere convertible	1991, top down, top up
MAD-8	1957	Lincoln Premiere 4dr Landau hardtop	1993

Durham Classics Automotive Miniatures

Durham Classics has not issued any new models since 2003. A Canadian company, Durham Classics Automobile Miniatures, has a loyal following. With over a dozen patterns ranging from a 1939 Ford panel truck to a 1954 Thunderbird prototype, the builder has successfully provided variations on its models in many different colours and liveries. A typical Durham Classics

Ford Motor Company models from Durham Classics

Number	Year	Marque/model	Comments
DC-2	1953	Ford pickup truck	Various versions
DC-3	1939	Ford panel van	Several liveries
DC-4	1938	Lincoln Zephyr club coupé	
DC-6	1953	Ford F-100 utility truck	Various versions including telephone company
DC-7	1954	Ford Courier sedan delivery	Many versions including Trans-Canada Air
DC-8/9	1938	Lincoln Zephyr convertible	Top up and top down
DC-13	1939	Ford panel delivery	Dual wheels. Extended body, various liveries
DC-14	1951	Ford Monarch 2dr sedan	
DC-15	1941	Ford coupé	Civilian & police versions
DC-20/21	1941	Ford convertible top up/top down	
DC-23	1939	Ford rail bus	One version fits on 'O' gauge track
DC-23A	1939	Ford bus	
DC-24	1954	Ford tow truck	
DC-25	1955	Ford pickup	
DC-36	1954	Ford Thunderbird prototype	Two-tone 'Fairlane' paint treatment
DC-37	1955	Ford panel van	

BUILDERS

model is built like a brick with great heft and deep glossy paint. Silver-foiled packaging resembles expensive boxed liquors. Model proportions and assembly quality are top rate. Durham, in later replicas, added details such as chrome door handles to keep pace with Brooklin and Motor City USA.

Expect to pay $125-$150 for new models in stores.

Margaret (and Julian) Stewart of Durham Classics: "Working from the basement of our home in the 1970s, the first models we produced for sale were 1934 Chrysler Airflow 2 door sedans. We took these to the big Canadian Toy Collectors' Society Show in the early 1980s. They looked a little bit like the old Dinky toys with balloon tires and no windows. I wish we could say that, at the start, people couldn't get enough of them but, at first, we didn't sell too many. Gradually, sales took off and we got quite a following. Julian was able to leave his employer and I was able to devote more time to running the hobby as a business.

"Incidentally, the first model made was the 1932 Packard Light 8. Julian applied his drafting and engineering knowledge (and artistry) by carving the mold out of a block of wood. He collaborated with long-time associate and fellow car model lover, John Hall, who made it one of his first models in the newly-founded Brooklin company. Eventually, John left Canada to set up shop in England. We stayed in Canada where Julian began to design his own casting machines and produce ever more sophisticated models such as the 1939 Ford panel van and 1953 Ford pickup.

"We enjoy models of cars and light trucks from the '30s to the '50s, and are especially proud of being chosen to provide historically accurate liveries to commemorate major collector events".

ENCHANTMENT LAND COACHBUILDERS

Enchantment Land Coachbuilders' (ELC) Jerry Rettig's passion for car models is evident the minute you talk to him. Jerry took one look at my car diorama website and immediately sent me examples of his fine models and dioramas. Fortunately, many of these pictures and extensive listings of thousands of models are available in Jerry's *American Wheels, a Reference*. This definitive publication provides many hours of enjoyment to those who love 1:43 scale model cars.

What about ELC models? Jerry has close to 100 standard models in his repertoire as well as many one-offs he has done during the years. ELC models offers a variety of body styles for Buicks, Chryslers, Cadillacs and Packards of the 1940s and 1930s, as well as a number of other cars. Jerry will rework die-cast models or produce body variations on familiar models such as limousines, ambulances and funeral cars.

Made from resin, ELC models may lack the heft of white metal models but have great proportions and a charm unto

1946 LIMOUSINE BY SIEBERT. HANDBUILT IN RESIN BY ENCHANTMENT LAND COACHBUILDERS WHICH SELDOM ISSUES MORE THAN 25 OF ANY ONE MODEL. (COURTESY J RETTIG)

themselves. ELC models are exclusive, with some numbering fewer than 10 items. They typically sell for $125-$150 and have a loyal following who like this artisan's work.

Says Bruce Arnold: "Jerry Rettig has one of the best jobs in the business. He can make a model of anything anyone wants, and probably has. Though not a player in the high dollar handbuilt arena, he has certainly amused and delighted many a collector. His models are cast by Richard Carlson Products of Arizona".

Jerry says: "I fooled around with models since I was a little kid, both model cars and trains. As I got older, like most young boys I switched my interest to real cars. Through the years I've had quite a few including hot rods, customs, special interest, and lots of daily drivers. About 30 years ago I visited Harrah's collection and was impressed and inspired. I knew I would never have the wherewithal to build a similar collection of real cars, but I thought perhaps something in miniature that would capture the flavor of Harrah's would be possible.

"Unfortunately, when I started collecting in earnest there were few models of American marque cars in 1:43 scale: a few Solidos, Rios, Dinkys, Corgis, and a couple of kits. Hence the start of conversions and modifications to create more models for my collection. A few folks saw what I was doing and wanted conversions done for their collections. This snowballed into Enchantment Land Coachbuilders and an ever increasing interest in 1:43 American model cars. As a result, we now have *American Wheels*, the creation of one model car enthusiast for all the others who aren't quite as crazy. My collection is now at about 2500 pieces and probably 20 per cent are one-off models (I really do like to build!), and continuing to grow as new models come to market.

"Mostly I build a particular model because I want it for my collection (for example the string of Indy pace cars). If the model turns out reasonably well and I think there may be a market for it, then I'll invest the time for custom molds, parts casting, plating,

Ford in miniature

Ford Motor Company models from Enchantment Land Coachbuilders

Number	Year	Marque/model	Comments
F-1	1950	Ford Meteor convertible top down	
F-2	1951	Ford Victoria 2dr hardtop	
F-3	1935	Ford Limousine hearse	Siebert
F-4	1935	Ford ambulance LWB	Siebert
L-1	1941	Lincoln Continental hardtop coupé	
L-12	1932	Lincoln Murphy roadster	Indy 500 pace car
M-2	1966	Mustang GT convertible	
M-5	1966	Mustang notchback coupé	
T-1	1960	Ford Thunderbird 2dr hardtop	
T-2	1965	Ford Thunderbird convertible top down	

etc, and bring a small group of models to market. My favorite ELC model? Probably the 37 Packard or 38 LaSalle art-carved hearses, or maybe the 28 Marmon roadster. It's hard to pick a favorite. The 37 Packard line was pretty much the start of ELC so nostalgia says that should be the one.

"What I have found very interesting is the number of models that have since been done of models that I first brought to market. Fortunately for the world of collectors, they are usually better than mine were! Motor City 66 Cadillac hearses and flower cars are fantastic, but also expensive. Brooklin now has a Muntz Jet in top down; my version is top up. Western now has a 41 Buick station wagon. Mostly, my models don't compete with the other manufacturers.

"My goal has been to provide odd-ball models that other manufacturers wouldn't find profitable. For example, a 25 Franklin, a 24 Cole, even a Kaiser Allstate, or a 1935 Ford funeral car by Siebert."

ECMA/Jeda 43

This French company is still issuing handbuilt models marketed under the Minicars 43 banner, and is still considered to be one of the best French handbult makers, with models that are a little more expensive than most. The maker issued a very nice 1948 Ford 2 door sedan, convertible and Sportsman, as well as a 1949 Mercury. These models are quite scarce.

Frobly

Another French company that produced a number of models during the late 1970s and early 1980s. Its 1961 Econoline is unique and 1951 Mercury convertible is fairly common, and not quite as detailed as the current Tin Wizard/Skyline.

Goldvarg

Sergio Goldvarg provided a full color brochure with models from his Goldvarg Collection. This photograph, taken from a Goldvarg brochure in the author's collection, shows a 1956 Premiere that the company did not issue. A shame, as this fully painted and detailed casting looks quite impressive. (Author collection)

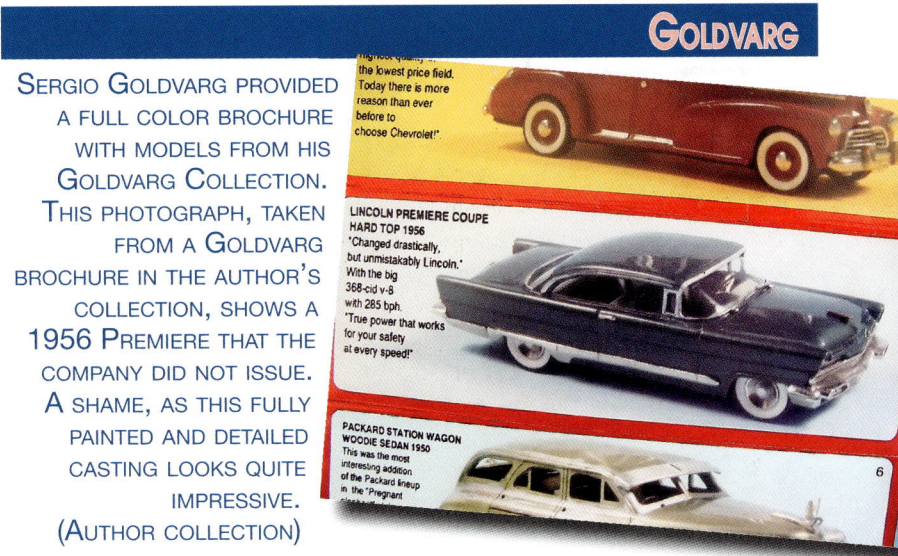

In the pantheon of handbuilt replicas, Goldvarg models were like Brooklin products: substantial, seemingly built from a chunk of white metal, with proportions and detailing that were impressionistic rather than exact replicas of the vehicle the models were based on.

Sergio and Mariana Goldvarg brought a love of mid-20th century automobiles to their native Argentina, where they set up shop and produced their first white metal creation, a 1957 Oldsmobile 98 Starfire 2 door hardtop. Soon, during the last decade of the twentieth century, they produced ten more models, including the 1955 Pontiac Star Chief convertible, a hard-to-find homely 1949 Plymouth Station Wagon, and a more sophisticated 1956 Mercury convertible, pictured in this book. Goldvarg also planned a 2 door hardtop version of the Mercury and a 1956 Lincoln Premiere, although neither was made.

However, Sergio's love of automobiles continues to this day. He is an occasional contributor to the 1:43 Bulletin Board on the Diecast Zone website, and had something to do with the original Lincoln Futura-based Batmobile being parked outside one of his Florida restaurants. Holy Handbuilts, Sergio, how did you manage to get that model?

Heitech

An Australian maker, Heitech released a small number of 1940 Ford 5 window coupé replicas (number 1) in 1:44 scale, and a few 1936 Ford convertible sedans with top up (number 2), and

BUILDERS

1936 Ford roadsters (number 3) in the early 1990s. The 1940 Ford is a simple but decent white metal handbuilt that was available in Folkestone Grey as well as a number of other original Ford colours.

LEGENDARY MOTORCARS LLC

Legendary is a small company owned by Joel Dickson which thus far has produced 1:43 scale white metal replicas of 1956-1969 North American luxury motorcars; notably Cadillac, Imperial, and Lincoln. Its 1969 Lincoln MkIII is available through a few suppliers and from Joel directly. The magnificent 1960 MkV convertible and hardtop coupé issued earlier are out of production and scarce. The 1956 Continental MkII is extremely detailed and exceptionally rare. Legendary's models were made by Illustra Models from excellent Ian Pickering patterns. The 1969 MkIIIs may be viewed on the Midlantic website (www.midlanticmodels.com).

MARQUE ONE

1958 FORD FAIRLANE SUNLINER TOP UP CONVERTIBLE BY MARQUE ONE MODELS, NUMBER 11. (AUTHOR COLLECTION)

This British builder handmade white metal and resin models during the 1980s. Like A&S, it had a very small range consisting of a 1949 Chrysler Town & Country convertible in both top up and top down configurations, a 1958 Ford Victoria 2 door hardtop, and a Sunliner convertible with top up or down.

All models had a resin body and white metal base. Proportions were very good, as was detail. While the resin on my Chrysler was not perfect, the models have some nice photo-etched metal parts for side moldings and vent windows. The grille on the Ford had a realistic and uniformly fine pattern, though the holes were too big. Early releases should not be considered comparable with current model standards.

MILESTONE MINIATURES LTD

Graham Du Cross' Milestone Miniatures of England makes several ranges of scale models which include a superb collection of Jaguar models, Gems and Cobwebs race cars; the Brooklands Series (produced in conjunction with the Brooklands Museum

FORD MOTOR COMPANY models from MILESTONE MINIATURES

NUMBER	YEAR	MARQUE/MODEL	COMMENTS
2	1960	FORD FALCON 4DR SEDAN	SOUTH AFRICAN MADE
9	1936	FORD 3 WINDOW COUPÉ	
13	1968	FORD TORINO FASTBACK	
18	1966	MERCURY CYCLONE GT 2DR HARDTOP	

Trust); the Milestone range of classic English cars, and the 43rd Avenue (FTA) range of classic American cars.

The company produces handbuilt models that it sells. It also undertakes contract work and commissions for other companies and collectors such as K&D Automobilia and Toys For Collectors (TFC).

MINICHAMPS

MINICHAMPS 1928 MODEL A WITH BLACK POLYSTYRENE DISPLAY BASE, CLEAR COVER AND PACKAGING. TODAY'S DIE-CAST MODEL COMPANIES OFTEN PROVIDE DURABLE PACKAGING THAT ALLOWS THE MODEL TO BE DISPLAYED IN A DUST-FREE ENVIRONMENT. (AUTHOR COLLECTION)

The producer of a seemingly inexhaustible supply of flawless, well-detailed and nicely constructed die-cast 1:43 scale models (mostly of European cars and trucks), this company is in this book for one reason: it makes some darned fine replicas of North American Ford Motor Company products.

Headquartered in Germany, with manufacturing in China, Minichamps was licensed by Ford to produce the centennial celebration 'Heart and Soul' series. Available at a reasonable $300, this set contained the following models: 1914 Ford Model T; 1928 Ford Model A; 1940 Ford DeLuxe Woody wagon; 1941 Lincoln Continental MkI; 1948 Ford F-1 pickup; 1949 Ford Custom convertible; 1950 Mercury Sport coupé; 1955 Ford Thunderbird; 1956 Lincoln Continental MkII; 1958 Edsel Bermuda station wagon; 1964 Ford Mustang; 1969 Mercury Marauder, and 2004 Ford GT. Many of these models, like the Model A and MkI pictured elsewhere, are still sold individually.

Ford in Miniature

Mini Marque '43' & Mini Marque

Midlantic Models, with Steve Overy, Mike Murray, Nick Hagley, and Clive Nye, and pattern making by Ian Pickering, acquired the patterns of Mini Marque '43' in 2004 and has since released former and new models under the 'Minimarque' name.

Mini Marque '43' was a prolific English producer of handbuilt replicas. Models from the '30s – Auburn, Cord, Duesenberg and Packard – are lovingly detailed with fine touches such as leather straps on the side-mounted spare wheels. Many of these models are in showcases of non-model collectors who find their accurate evocation of a bygone era irresistible.

The company ceased production in 2002 when its founder, the flamboyant Richard Briggs, passed away. In 2004, Mini Marque was resurrected by Midlantic Models with the issue of a 1956 Packard 400 hardtop and 1946 Hudson coupé, using components from the original Mini Marque '43' patterns. Mini Marque '43' models retailed at between $175-$275; their aftermarket value has yet to stabilize. Early indications are that '50s models are less coveted but Duesenbergs and 'Cars of the Stars' are in demand and priced accordingly.

The company made some fine models of Ford Motor Company products from 1936 and 1957-59. I particularly like the 1957 Ford line that had a 2 door station wagon, Ranchero, convertible and 2 door hardtop. The convertibles are quite common. Try to get the later releases because they have more detail. Excellent 1957 Mercury Turnpikes, 1958 Edsels, and 1959 Lincoln models were made as well.

Mini Marque plans to issue a 1958 Edsel Citation 4 door hardtop sedan, based on the earlier 2 door pattern, in 2006.

Bruce Arnold has this to say: "There is no-one on earth like Richard Briggs. Since he departed this earthly coil no-one has taken his place. By hook or by crook, Richard made model after model, never knowing if it would be his last. He alone pioneered the beginnings of the 1:43 fully finished model world.

"He had a great eye for Americana, and even owned several American Cars. He traveled the US like an itinerant preacher, saving souls from the trunk of his car. First to Dave Sinclair's Mini Auto and then to the many other dealers that have since closed in the face of $200 hand-builts.

"A most unusual trait was Richard's narcolepsy. He would excuse himself abruptly in the middle of a conversation to sit down for a 5 minute nap. The whole Mini Marque '43' story has yet to be told. Richard wrote his whole history down in correspondence with me with permission for it to be published one day."

Now that's a book I'd buy!

Mini Marque '43' Mercury Turnpikes astride their boxes. Through the years the company has made its packaging more colorful as the light blue and red box on the right attests, but Richard Briggs' beloved bull terrier, Cilla, endured as mascot and company logo. Each Mini Marque '43' model also had a decal of Cilla on its base. (Author collection)

Ford Motor Company models from Mini Marque '43'

Number	Year	Marque/model	Comments
US-5A	1958	Edsel Citation convertible	
US-5B	1958	Edsel Citation hardtop	
US-45B	1935	Ford V-8 convertible sedan	
RP-4	1935	Ford convertible sedan	Indy 500 pace car
US-6D	1936	Ford V8 convertible 4dr sedan	
US-6A	1936	Ford V-8 roadster	
US-6C	1936	Ford V-8 sedan delivery	Various liveries
CS-14A	1937	Ford station wagon	Clark Gable car
US-19	1957	Ford Del Rio ranch wagon	
US-2A	1957	Ford Fairlane 500 convertible	Top up, top down and two-tone
US-2D	1957	Ford Fairlane 500 Victoria hardtop coupé	Two-tone, continental wheel
US-20	1957	Ford Ranchero pickup	
US-36	1959	Lincoln Continental Conv	
US-26C	1964	Lincoln Continental 4dr hardtop	
US-26	1964	Lincoln Continental Conv	
RP-2	1957	Mercury Turnpike Cruiser convertible	Indy 500 pace car
US-21A	1957	Mercury Turnpike Cruiser convertible	
US-21B	1957	Mercury Turnpike Cruiser hardtop	
US-40	1958	Thunderbird convertible	Top up, top down, continental kit
US-41B	1958	Thunderbird hardtop	

BUILDERS

Motor City USA

For serious collectors of handbuilt American model cars, Alan Novak's Motor City USA is the pinnacle of excellence.

Motor City USA produces four lines of models in 1:43: Top-of-the-Line street models such as the 1956 Oldsmobile 98 referred to by collectors as 'Full Motor City'; professional cars in the 'Sunset Coach' line with models like the 1966 Cadillac Superior ambulance; entry-level 'American Models' line with its 1939 Ford Woody wagon, and 'Design Studio' rods and customs. All Motor City USA models are flawlessly proportioned, carefully detailed, and perfectly assembled and finished. Each is a precision piece with phenomenal attention to detail and authenticity. Other things that set the builder's products apart are that delicate parts such as aerials and mirrors seldom break or fall off, and the range of colours offered is amazing. All models retain their value and many appreciate in value. Motor City USA Models range from $135-$300 in price.

1955 Mercury Sun Valley Design Studios model number DS-10 and 1955 Ford Crown Victoria Skyliner model number MC-10S. (Author collection)

Ford Motor Company models from Motor City USA

American Models line

Number	Year	Marque/model	Comments
AM-1	1939	Ford Woody wagon	

Design Studio line

(Early in Motor City USA's history, top-of-the-line models were named Design Studio. Eventually, this name was used for the current rod and custom line.)

9C	1940	Ford 5 window coupé	
9D	1940	Ford convertible	Top down
9U	194	Ford convertible	Top up
10	1955	Mercury Sun valley 2dr hardtop coupé	Transparent roof panel
10C	1955	Mercury Montclair convertible	
10H	1955	Mercury Montclair 2dr hardtop coupé	

Top-of-the-Line line

10	1950	Ford convertible	
11	1950	Ford Club coupé	
12	1950	Ford 2 Dr. sedan	
13	1950	Ford station wagon	
14	1950	Ford 4dr sedan	
14P	1950	Ford 4dr sedan police	LAPD
15	1955	Ford Sunliner convertible	
16	1955	Ford Crown Victoria	
16S	1955	Ford Crown Victoria Skyliner	
51	1951	Ford Victoria 2dr hardtop	
52	1951	Ford convertible	
56	1947	Ford Sportsman convertible	
64	1955	Lincoln Capri convertible	
65	1955	Lincoln Capri 2dr hardtop	
72	1947	Ford Woody station wagon	
74	1952	Lincoln 2dr hardtop	
75	1953	Lincoln convertible	

USA Models line

USA-8	1940	Ford 4dr sedan	
USA-9	1940	Ford 4dr sedan	Yellow Cab
USA-10	1940	Ford 4dr sedan	LAPD
USA-11	1940	Ford 2dr sedan	
USA-12	1940	Ford 4dr sedan	Army staff
USA-13	1940	Ford 4dr sedan	Fire Chief
USA-14	1940	Ford pickup	
USA-15	1940	Ford convertible	Top down
USA-16	1940	Ford club coupé	
USA-17	1951	Ford Crestliner	
USA-23	1955	Mercury Sun Valley 2dr hardtop	
USA-24	1955	Mercury Monterey convertible	
USA-28	1955	Ford Sunliner convertible	
USA-37	1937	Ford Flat Back 2dr sedan	
USA-38	2000	Ford Thunderbird	
USA-41	1948	Ford Convertible	
USA-43	1940	Ford LAPD Police Deptartment tow truck	Limited edition
USA-44	1940	Ford LAPD Fire Deptartment tow truck	Limited edition of 200

Ford in Miniature

Nostalgic Miniatures

An early and long-since departed inhabitant of the handbuilt model arena was this company from Westborough, Massachusetts, USA, which produced close to two dozen different Ford miniatures as well as dozens of other marque replicas. Made mostly from pewter (even the wheels), the replicas exemplify early efforts by fledgling companies to capture the appearance of the original subject: in other words (and in my opinion), the proportions of Nostalgic Miniatures' replicas tend to be a little impressionistic rather than absolutely accurate. Details are also modest with each model comprising fewer parts than in today's replicas. Built-up models from this company – with the exception of the 1930 Ford and the 1955-56 Thunderbird – appear hard to come by, although it seems easier to acquire bare pewter replicas. The 1941 Lincoln Continental coupé, the only extant subject, looks better than the others.

Oakland Models

Now defunct, this American builder produced a smattering of 1940, 1950, 1953 and 1954 Ford Motor Company models from the late 1970s to the early 1980s. Its line overlaps that of Auto Buff which sold a number of its patterns to Oakland; Zaugg Models also used its patterns. The 1950 sedan is well done and the 1954 Skyliner and Sunliner are worth collecting. These models appear infrequently on the aftermarket.

Precision Miniatures

Precision Miniatures was one of the pioneers in the handbuilt model field whose models – whilst Gene Parrill and Lloyd Asbury were at the helm – were of a consistently high calibre. Canadian patternmaker, Dick Armbruster, made the bodies of several PM models from wood, with Lloyd creating the delicate brass details. A number of these models, such as the 1952 Hudson Hornet and 1953 Lincoln Capri, formed the basis of later Motor City USA releases, demonstrating that a great pattern can endure, though the Hudson is overscale.

Other Precision Miniatures models were: 1956 Chrysler New Yorker hardtop and convertible; 1953 Corvette; 1952 Cunningham race car; 1932 Duesenberg SJ Weymann speedater, and 1964-66 Ford Mustang convertible and fastback which also included a Shelby GT 350 version.

Says Gene Parrill "I started Marque Products, a retailer of 1:43 scale cars, in 1972 in Costa Mesa, California. In 1975 I met Lloyd Asbury, a master model-maker, and we put together Precision Miniatures. The purpose was to bring out kits that filled various niches that were being overlooked.

"Our first products were Indy cars. These were very complicated to build and the market wasn't very big. We then brought out a few Porsches kits which sold much better. It was at this point that we decided to start bringing out American car models. I was still running Marque Products along with my mom and dad, and doing the business side of PM. Lloyd was doing the casting during the day and working on masters in the evening.

"We soon determined that we couldn't bring out new kits fast enough unless Lloyd worked on masters full time. So we hired someone to do the casting and someone else to package the kits.

"We heard about a Canadian named Dick Armbruster who could make masters for us so we commissioned him to start work on the Duesenberg. He went on to make three or four masters for us before he gave it up to do masters for Julian Stewart, a fellow Canadian.

"In 1979 I had an offer to sell Marque Products and I did. I saw that Precision Miniatures was not making enough money to support both Lloyd and me so I put my half up for sale. Doug Johnson came along and bought my half then made an offer to purchase Lloyd's half as well. Doug ran the business for a year or two selling built-up PM models. He then sold the masters and went out of business. Lloyd went on to start his own model shop and I went back into the mainframe computer business.

"I, of course, keep my hand in the hobby. Until recently, I moderated the Forum 43 Discussion Board on the Diecast Zone website (www.diecast.org)."

Ford Motor Company models from Precision Miniatures

Number	Year	Marque/model	Comments
231	1953	Lincoln Capri 2dr hardtop	
232	1953	Lincoln Capri Top down convertible	Available with Santa Claus driver
18	1964	Mustang Top down convertible	Also pace car version
19	1965	Mustang 2+2 Fastback	
20	1965	Mustang 2+2 Fastback Shelby GT 350	
21	1966	Mustang 2+2 Fastback Shelby GT 350	
22	1965	Mustang Notchback coupé	

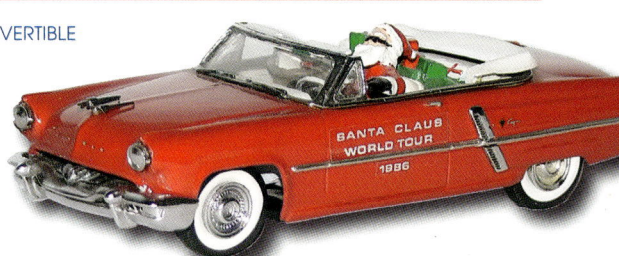

1953 Lincoln Capri convertible Santa Claus World Tour from 1988. 1 of 350 built. Precision Miniatures. PM-232. (Courtesy A. Thomas)

Builders

Rextoys

Rextoys of Portugal published a full color brochure that had many skillful line art illustrations of its models, present and intended. The 1935 Ford atop a brochure from the author's collection was released in many different body styles, colors, and liveries. (Author collection)

According to its 1980s brochure, Count Giansante Coluzzi, Rextoys' president, wished to "create a 'museum' of dream cars, living proof of what was the great era of the Automobile, historically, individually, and, of course, artistically."

This now defunct Portuguese company did choose some interesting, well-proportioned and well-constructed die-cast subjects such as a '38 Cadillac and '39 Packard. Noteworthy if only for its audacity, the 'Cicciolina Cadillac' featured the topless figure of the Italian porn star/MP, Cicciolina.

Rextoys manufactured several 1935 Fords, such as a Fordor, Tudor, station wagon, and sedan delivery. Though the paintwork is not up to latest standard, good models are readily available on the aftermarket at a reasonable price.

Sun Motor Company

No, the model is not a Ford, but behind this Sun Models DeSoto is a Sun 1970 Mustang Boss 302 fastback. This replica was originally made with a white metal body, and then later in resin as repeat production quantities became smaller. Total production amounted to 500 pieces, 400 in resin. (Author collection)

This England-based builder handmade white metal and resin car models during the 1980s. Its only American car models were the fairly plentiful white metal 1947 De Soto Suburban model, available also as hearse, ambulance, and taxi, the less-common Ertl-based 1952 Cadillac S75 7 passenger sedan, and the rare 1970 Ford Mustang fastback later released by Boss Models. Having owned examples of the first two models, I can comment that, though sturdy and well-proportioned, they lacked the detail of today's handbuilts.

The originator of Sun Models is the well-known and knowledgeable enthusiast Rod Ward, editor of *Model Auto Review*. Rod sells Sun Models and a variety of other 1:43 models from his on-line store, Modelauto.

Says Rod: "Our first models were 'dinky repros' such as the Veteran and Vintage Models (Vic Bailey) range from Brighton, and the De Soto and Bristol 450 ex AGM-Geoff Moorhouse (who originally made them in resin, but we retooled for white metal). Geoff made our Humber Super Snipe and Mustang, and Alan Smith began our truck range for us. We then went on to employ other pattern makers to make original cars such as the Bentley, Caddy stretch, etc, and trucks. We bought Denis Baudet's French DB range which formed the core of our Bugattiana range. Then we bought Gérard Daninden's French range (Epoit and Belle Epoque) to form the core of the Rapide range and moved all the other cars into that range from Sun.

"The Sun range continued to grow very large – lots of trucks, fire appliances, etc, but we ran into problems getting built models made to an adequate standard (all our work was done by subcontractors), and could then only sell kits, reducing our potential market. We had success with our fourth range – Bijou – which concentrated on odd-ball kits and transkits, but the recent clampdown on licensing meant we'd have to pay license fees on transkits (even though the 'base models' already had fees paid on them) which would make new projects economically unviable, as production runs are so short for transkits. So production halted for a while. The Bijou range included some products based on Auto Replicas and Scottoy items, bought in from them.

"As the overall market contracted, we have sold parts of the ranges: a lot of the Rapide and Bugattiana ranges to CCC of France, where we thought that Georges Pont would do a superb job, as he has. We also ran into some perplexing issues of seeing our products surfacing elsewhere under different names (it's cheaper to make a resin copy of someone else's product than to invest in a completely new pattern), so we thought we could let Georges sort that out closer to home. Alan Smith took over production of some of our trucks in his range, then Hartsmith models stopped building, though I believe he has started up again on a smaller scale.

"Currently we have no production and are only selling from remaining stock, but we are always looking at other projects."

Ford in miniature

Tin Wizard

Tin Wizard is Germany's builder of fine handbuilt car models, in business for many years and the producer of several American car models (under the Skyline name) which were formerly made by defunct builder, Zaugg/Empire Models.

I note that the builder currently produces only the better models that Jörg Zaugg once produced; these come in a wide range of colors and are nicely detailed and finished.

Owner Thomas Wolter says: "We are lovers of cars and do not accept compromise where models are concerned. Mass-production of industrially manufactured models is not appropriate for us. Therefore, we only manufacture small series aiming to have detailing faithful to the original cars.

"There is a remarkable difference between us and the 'Big Boys': we are a small firm concentrating on manufacturing in a craftsman style and to an exceptional standard. Before a new type goes into 'series' production, we make the pattern of the model manually in a process that can take weeks. We use mainly the standard 1:43 scale which allows the smallest vehicle details to be excellently represented.

"It is not sufficient for us to manufacture perfect models; you want to possess an accurate mirror image of the car, therefore we use a special tin alloy for the casting, and test and examine many sample castings to ensure the ideal casting conditions.

"Only then can the model go into production. A mold is enough for approximately 300 models and is then destroyed The cast parts are now cleaned individually by hand and painted. We use 2-pack auto paint mixed to ensure a match to the original color.

"With much care and patience our co-workers then install the prepared cast parts, as well as applying decals and fitting photo-etched parts made from German silver with turned parts made from brass and aluminum. The assembly process can take up to two or three hours for each model. Finally, using a fine brush made with red deer hair, details are painted by hand. You may, however, opt to purchase a kit that you can assemble yourself for a personal touch."

1963 Thunderbird 2 door hard top coupé. Tin Wizard model number TW-505-1. (Courtesy Tin Wizard)

Ford Motor Company models from Tin Wizard

Number	Year	Marque/model	Comments
TW-501	1950	Mercury 2dr coupé	
TW-502	1950	Mercury 2dr coupé	Fire Department of New York
TW-503	1950	Mercury Top down convertible	
TW-504	1950	Mercury Top down convertible	Indianapolis 500 pace car
TW-505	1961	Ford Thunderbird	Top down convertible
TW-506	1961	Ford Thunderbird	Top down convertible roadster with tonneau cover
TW-508	1961	Ford Thunderbird	Top down convertible Indianapolis pace car

Western Models Ltd

Western Models has produced fine models for three decades, under its own banner and for other companies, including Motor City USA, Design Studio, TFC, and EWA. Offering a broad range of American street models, it has been particularly careful to issue models in the prosaic, but popular, 4 door sedan and station wagon body styles.

Lately, Western has issued a number of 1940s models, including Woody wagon versions of the 1941-42 Buick and Hudson, '41 Packard Clipper, '41 Oldsmobile 4 door sedan and '48 Lincoln 2 and 4 door sedans.

This builder is also well-known for its assortment of late 1950s sedans, hardtops and convertibles, including Ford and Edsel models.

Western Models offerings are mid-priced, positioned between Brooklin and Motor City USA. The models are accurate in scale and well-detailed with chrome door handles and photo-etched wipers. To keep costs down, emblems are usually decals and interiors are simple.

Western's models cost $150 brand new. Aftermarket prices tend to range widely and typically match the model's original issue price.

Mike Stephens of Western Models says: "The company was incorporated in October of 1973 from humble beginnings literally at the bottom of our garden. The garage served as the first workshop of Western Models for 18 months.

"Our first model was a Mercedes Benz 540K released in January 1974 at the now well-known Windsor Swap Meet. Our first customer for the Mercedes Benz 540K was the Lang brothers of Danhausen in Germany, and many models have been produced for them over the following 10 years, as well as Western's own comprehensive range. Gunter Lang went on to

Builders

WESTERN MODELS LIMITED 1959 EDSEL AND 1959 FAIRLANE ATOP THEIR WESTERN AND SMALL WHEELS BOXES. BEHIND THEM IS A SHEET DEPICTING A SMALL SAMPLE OF THE PROLIFIC BUILDERS' MODELS. (AUTHOR COLLECTION)

produce the now-famous Minichamps range in China, of which Western produced some early examples.

"From the beginning, we strived for quality and attention to detail. As a result, the demand for our handmade metal scale models has allowed Western Models to expand throughout our history. Having started in Epsom, Surrey from an idea originally planned in Devon, the company moved to various larger premises, first in Redhill, Surrey, and then a major move back west to Taunton. At present based in a rural setting, the company has gone back to its 'western' roots.

"During the 1970s and '80s, a strong link was forged with many F1 teams and models were produced in lots of different scales from 1:87 through to 1:4 original size. In Taunton a new range of aircraft was started in 1:200 scale and this now represents 50 per cent of Western Models' production.

"As for model cars, we have produced replicas of both European and American automobiles for many years, including models of lower-line cars such as the 1958 Ford 300, an example of which I once owned.

"Western Models undertakes the complete production process from drawings, through origination to final articles. This includes spin casting of different alloys, vacforming, artwork and design.

"Our family craft business employs 10 staff and helps Joyce and I to continue producing high quality metal models for discerning collectors."

Ford Motor Company models from Western Models Limited

American models – WMS

Number	Year	Marque/model	Comments
WMS46	1959	Ford Skyliner Retractable top up	Continental wheel
WMS46X	1959	Ford Fairlane convertible open	Continental wheel
WMS53	1959	Ford Ranchero pickup	Various door logos
WMS74	1955	Lincoln Capri 2dr hardtop	
WMS74X	1955	Lincoln Capri convertible open	
WMS77	1946	Ford sedan	
WMS77P	1946	Ford sedan Police	Missouri State Police
WMS77T	1946	Ford sedan taxi	
WMS80	1965	Ford Mustang convertible open	
WMS82	1959	Ford Country Squire station wagon	
WMS83	1948	Lincoln sedan	
WMS89	1959	Edsel Corsair sedan	

American models – small wheels

Number	Year	Marque/model	Comments
SW10	1967	Ford Mustang Notchback coupé	
SW17	1958	Ford Custom 300 4dr sedan	
SW17F	1958	Ford Custom 300 4dr sedan Fire Chief	Philadelphia Fire Department
SW17T	1958	Ford Custom taxi	
SW21	1959	Ford Fairlane 4dr sedan	
SW21P	1959	Ford Fairlane 4dr sedan Police	

Zaugg/Empire Models

Swiss builder, Jörg Zaugg, produced several models in white metal, many of which continue to be produced by Tin Wizard. The only Ford product no longer produced is the 1958 Edsel Pacer (hardtop coupé and convertible). I applaud this model because it is of the shorter wheelbase, lower-priced Pacer. Proportions were superb but the model was a little on the small size at around 1:45 scale, and many examples had a warped body. It also had sprung suspension which, whilst interesting, was reminiscent of a Corgi toy (and at five times the price!). Nonetheless, Mr Zaugg was a pioneer in the handbuilt model field and left us with many interesting, finely crafted scale models.

Suppliers 6

Because of their low sales volume, handbuilt models are sold by only a small number of companies. Shown on the maps are a number of reputable suppliers well known to collectors.

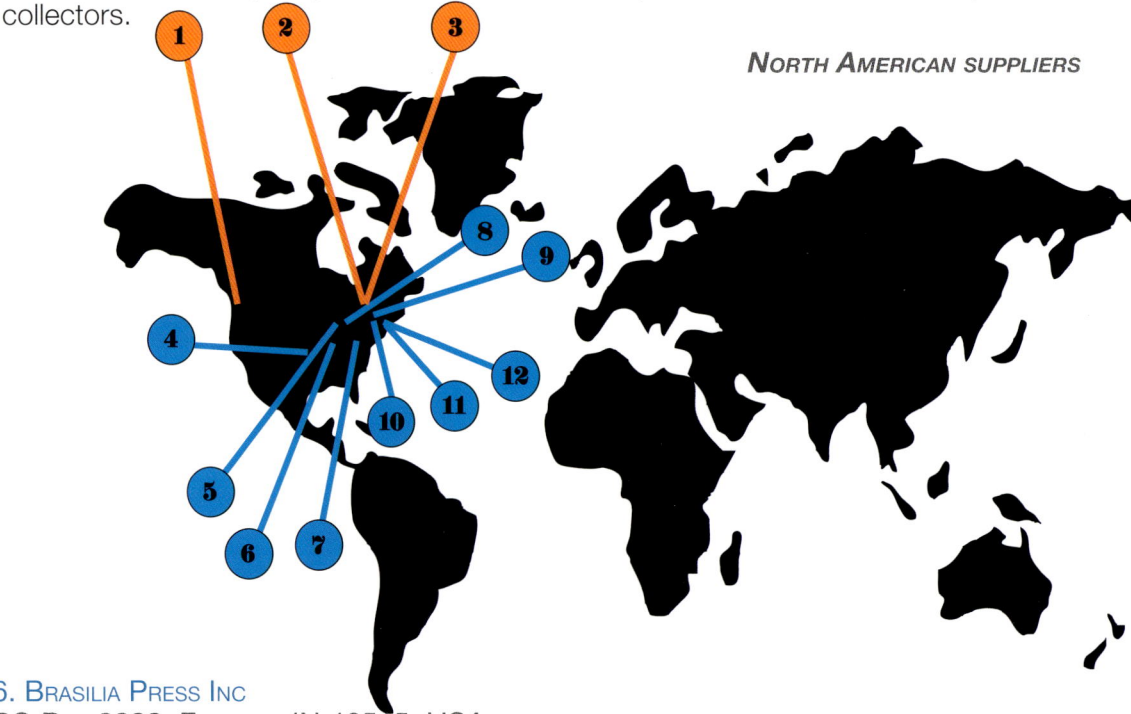

North American suppliers

1. eAutomobilia
2531 Ontario St, Vancouver,
BC V5T 2X7 Canada
Phone: 604 873 6242 Fax: 604 873 6259
info@eautomobilia.com
www.eautomobilia.com

2. Karmodels.com
7252 Vanness, Montreal, Quebec
H1S 1Y7, Canada
Phone: 514 255 8469
info@karmodels.com www.karmodels.com

3. Bibliauto
1524 Notre-Dame ouest, Montréal,
Quebec, Canada
Phone: 514 938 9399
bibliauto@bellnet.ca www.bibliauto.com

4. Motor City Kansas
8663 W Central, Wichita, KS 67212,
USA Phone: 316 945 1000
www.motorcityks.com

5. Route66modelstore.com
PO Box 145, Western Springs
IL 60558, USA
Phone: 708 246 1543 Fax: 708 246 1085
buz@route66modelcarstore.com
www.route66modelcarstore.com

6. Brasilia Press Inc
PO Box 2023, Elkhart, IN 46515, USA
Fax: 574 262 8799 www.brasiliapress.com

7. Dominion Models
PO Box 515, Salem, VA 24153, USA
Phone/fax: 540 375 3750
dominionmodels@aol.com

8. Sinclair's Mini-Auto
PO Box 8403, Erie, PA 16505, USA
Phone: 814 838 2274 Fax: 814 838 2274
dave@miniauto.com www.miniauto.com

9. Toys for Collectors
95 Public Square, Suite 511, Watertown,
NY 13601, USA
Toll free: 888 445 3322
Phone: 315 782 4692 Fax: 315 782 8167
tfcusa@northweb.com www.tfcusa.com

SUPPLIERS

10. LILLIPUT MOTOR CAR COMPANY
PO Box 145, Clarksburg, NJ 08510, USA
Phone: 732 446 9381 Fax: 732 446 9297
raypazjr@aol.com

11. EWAcars
205 US HWY 22, Green Brook, NJ 08812, USA
Phone: 732 424 7811 Fax: 732 424 7814
www.ewacars.com

12. ACCENT MODELS
PO Box 295, Denville, NJ 0783, USA
Phone: 973 887 8403 Fax: 973 887 5088
info@accentmodels.com
www.accentmodels.com

EUROPEAN & AUSTRALIAN SUPPLIERS

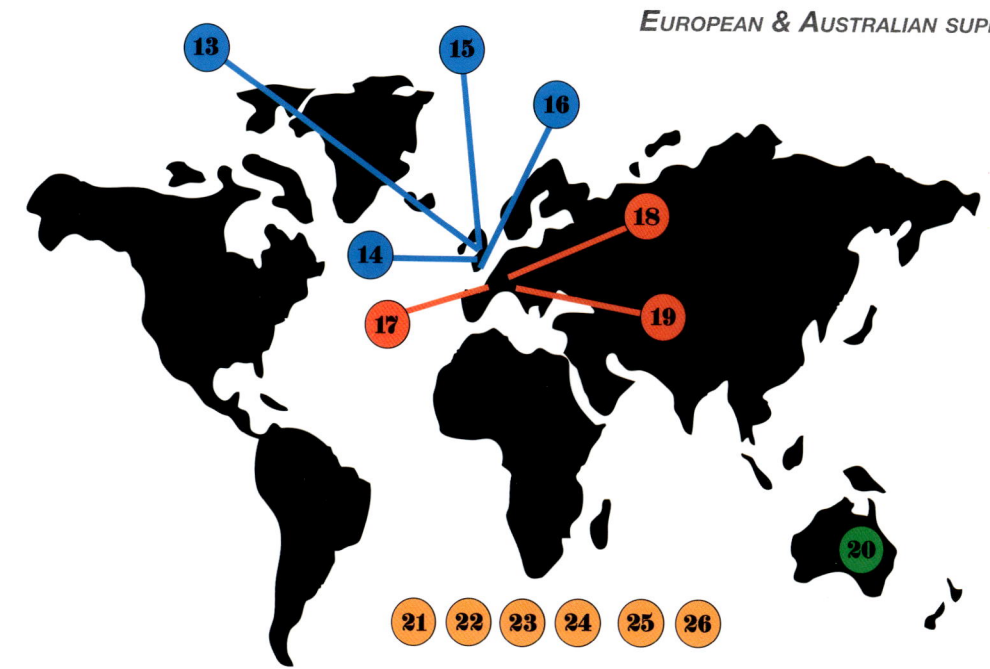

13. MODEL AUTO LTD
PO Box SM2, Leeds LS25 5XA, England
Phone: 01977 681966
Fax: 01977 681991
Sales@zeteo.com www.zeteo.com/mar

14. J M TOYS LTD
32 Aston Road, Waterlooville, Hampshire PO7 7XQ, England
Phone: 023 9226 2446
Fax: 023 9225 2041
sales@jmtoys.net www.jmtoys.net

15. SPACROFT
98 High Street, Tibshelf, Derby DE55 5NU, England
Phone: 01773 872780
spacroft@aol.com
www.spacroftmodels.co.uk

16. ST MARTINS MODEL CARS
95 St Martins Lane, London WC2N 4AS, England
Phone: 020 7836 9742
Fax: 020 7240 1219
www.stmartinsmodelcars.co.uk

17. SPIEL & HOBBY KUPSCH
Kardinal-Galen-Str 120, D47058 Duisburg, Germany
Phone: 203 28 2690 Fax: 203 28 8106
Pkupsch@kupsch-germany.com
www.kupsch-germany.de

18. AUTOSHOW
Roegergasse 18, A1090 Vienna Austria
Phone: 1-31 99 863
autoshow@aon.at www.autoshow.at

19. CAR43
4 Avenue Pictet de Rochemont CH-1207 Geneve, Switzerland
Phone: 022 736 84 90
Fax: 022 736 84 90
car43@bluewin.ch www.car43.ch

20. MODEL CARS OF THE WORLD
39 Benwerrin Drive
Burwood East, Victoria 3151 Australia
Phone: 3 9887 9929 Fax: 3 9887 8336
sales@modelcars.com.au
www.modelcars.com.au

An excellent source of models is eBay.com. Look under the Brooklin or Diecast Cars & Trucks section for:

21. Booshmama
22. 2cv01 (www. 2cv01.com)
23. Chadsworth (www.stores.ebay.com/brooklinandbritishmodelautoco)
24. Hobie48
25. Boxer Toys
26. Toyboy
(Alan Wank's website is: http://members.aol.com/awtoyboy/awtoyboy.html)

Why not visit Veloce on the web? – www.velocebooks.com
New book news • Special offers • Details of all books in print • Gift vouchers

Contact Details
Appendix 1

Ashton Models
www.feudal.cz/html/ashton_models/

BBR
www.bbrmodels.it/indexuk.htm

Brooklin Models
Brooklin Models Ltd, Pinesway Industrial Estate, IVO Peters Road, Bath BA2 3QS, England. www.brooklinmodels.co.uk
Phone: +44 (0)1225 332400
Facsimile: +44 (0)1225 447430
E-mail: brooklin_models@talk21.com

Conquest Madison
Conquest and Madison Models are now owned by Dave 'Buz' Kirkel of Route 66 Model Store.
Mail: PO Box 145
Western Springs
IL 60558, USA
Web: www.Route66modelcarstore.com
phone: 708 246 1543
Fax: 708 246 1085
E-mail: buz@route66modelcarstore.com

Enchantment Land Coachbuilders
2985 N. Walnut Avenue
Tucson, Az 85712, USA
E-mail: jerryrettig@msn.com

Legendary Motorcars LLC
Joel Dickson
Ocean City, USA
phone: 609 399 2401
E-mail: legendarymotorcars@hotmail.com

Milestone Miniatures
Milestone Miniatures Ltd
25 West End
Redruth
Cornwall, TR15 2SA
UK
Phone: 01209 218356
Fax: 01209 217983
E-mail: gemscobwebs@freeuk.com
Web: www.modelcars.co.uk

Minichamps
www.Minichamps.com

Mini Marque '43'
Phone: 0142 472 2007
Web: www.midlanticmodels.com

Motor City USA
13400 Saticoy Street #12
North Hollywood, California 91605, USA
E-mail: info@motorcityusa.com
Phone: 818.503.4835
Fax: 818.503.4580
Web: www.MotorCityUSA.com

Sun Motor Company
Web: www.zeteo.com/mar/
e-mail: sales@zeteo.com

Tin Wizard
Thomas Wolter Modelltechnik
Talstrasse 170
69198 Schriesheim, Germany
Phone: 06203 68 68 0
Fax: 06203 68 32 9
Web: www.tinwizard.de

Western Models Limited
Acre Ridge
Clayhidon
Nr Cullompton
Devon, EX15 3TW
England
Phone: +44 (0) 1823 666767
Fax: + 44 (0) 1823 666757
E-mail: sales@western-models.co.uk
Web: www.western-models.co.uk

Fords from 1928 to 1959: Minichamps 1928 Model A, USA Model 1937 Deluxe, Design Studios 1940 Deluxe, and Western Models 1959 Fairlane. (Author collection)

Photo Credits
Appendix 2

Fellow enthusiasts, suppliers, and builders endowed this book with their photographs. Here are the sources of the photos, contact information and/or websites:

Bruce Arnold Models
Bruce Arnold
465 Ridge Road
Novato
California 94947, USA
phone: 415 892 9588
Fax: 415 898 8213
e-mail: info@brucearnoldmodels.com

John Arnold

Henk van Asten

DMP Studios
Dean Paolucci
e-mail: modelcrafters@cogeco.ca

Durham Classics Automotive Miniatures
Julian and Margaret Stewart

Enchantment Land Coachbuilders
Jerry Rettig
2985 N Walnut Avenue,
Tucson, Az 85712, USA
E-mail: jerryrettig@msn.com

Minichamps 1928 Model A and Fleer Collectibles 1941 Ford.
(Author collection)

Andrew Thomas of www.lincolndownunder.com is a Lincoln authority with a huge model collection. A true artist, he modifies and scratch-builds Lincoln models to create entirely new replicas.
(Courtesy A Thomas)

Mini Marque '43' 1957 Ford Del Rio Ranch Wagon and American Models 1939 Ford station wagon. (Author collection)

EWAcars
205 US Hwy 22, Green Brook, NJ 08812, USA
phone: 732 424 0200
www.ewacars.com

Jim Hartman

David Larsen

Dirk Mathyssen

Alex Moskalev

John Roberts
e-mail: john.roberts@jrcustombuilt.com
www.jrcustombuilt.com

Andrew Thomas
e-mail: atd@netconnect.com.au
www.Lincolndownunder.com

Tin Wizard
Thomas Wolter Modelltechnik
Talstrasse 170, D-69198 Schriesheim, Germany
phone: 06203 68 68 0
fax 06203 68 32 9
www.tinwizard.de

Toys for Collectors
toll free number: 888 445 3322
e-mail: tfcusa@northweb.com
www.tfcusa.com

Western Models Ltd
Acre Ridge, Clayhidon, Nr Cullompton, Devon EX15 3TW, England
phone: 01823 666767
e-mail: sales@western-models.co.uk
www.western-models.co.uk

INDEX

MODELS
EDSEL CONVERTIBLE
    CITATION (1958) 58, 59
    PACER (1958) 59
    RANGER (1960) 62
EDSEL COUPÉ HARDTOP
    CITATION (1958) 58, 59
    PACER (1958) 59
EDSEL SEDAN CORSAIR (1959) 59, 117
EDSEL STATION WAGON BERMUDA (1958) 59

FORD BUS (1939) 22
FORD CABRIOLET (1933) 19
    (1936) 20
FORD CLUB COUPÉ (1941) 27
FORD CLUB COUPÉ (1949) 33
    COUPÉ CUSTOM (1950) 8, 33, 35
    COUPÉ DELUXE (1948) 28
FORD CONVERTIBLE (1948) 27
    CUSTOM (1950) 8, 35, 37
    CUSTOM DELUXE (1951) 8, 39, 40, 42
    DELUXE (1940) 21, 24, 25
    GALAXIE 500 (1963) 63
    PHAETON (1936) 9, 14, 20, 21
    RETRACTABLE SKYLINER (1959) 60, 61
    SPORTSMAN (1947) 27
    SUNLINER (1955) 47, 48, 49
    SUNLINER (1957) 51, 52, 53
    SUNLINER (1958) 57, 111
    SUNLINER (1959) 60
    SUNLINER (1960) 16, 61, 62
FORD COUPÉ (1932 & 1934) 18
    (1935) 20
    (1936) 20
    (1940) 24
    DELUXE (1940) 15, 24, 25, 26
    HARDTOP CRESTLINE VICTORIA (1954) 44
FORD COUPÉ HARDTOP FAIRLANE (1956) 50
    HARDTOP FAIRLANE (1957) 4, 51, 52, 53
    HARDTOP GALAXIE (1964) 64
    HARDTOP VICTORIA (1951) 8, 35, 40, 41, 42
    HARDTOP VICTORIA (1953) 45
    MODEL A (1928) 14, 18, 111
    MODEL A (1930) 17
FORD CROWN VICTORIA SKYLINER (1955) 6, 47, 48, 49, 113
FORD FALCON (1960) 63
    CONVERTIBLE FUTURA (1963) 64
    HARDTOP COUPÉ SPRINT (1963) 63, 64
    STATION WAGON (1963) 64

FORD FAIRLANE (1966) 67
FORD FORDOR HARDTOP SEDAN GALAXIE (1966) 64, 65
    SEDAN (1935) 19, 114
    SEDAN (1940) 26
    SEDAN (1946) 28, 29
    SEDAN (1947) 29
    SEDAN (1956) 50
    SEDAN 300 (1958) 58
    SEDAN CUSTOM (1950) 8, 15, 33, 35, 36
    SEDAN DELUXE (1951) 41, 42
    SEDAN FAIRLANE (1959) 60, 117
    SEDAN LWB (1936) 21, 104
    SEDAN STANDARD (1940) 15, 25, 26
FORD LIMOUSINE HEARSE SIEBERT (1935) 19
    SIEBERT (1940) 24
FORD LIMOUSINE SIEBERT (1946) 109
FORD MONARCH (1949) 42
    MONARCH (1951) 42
    MONARCH (1957) 53
FORD MUSTANG CONVERTIBLE (1965) 66, 67
    CONVERTIBLE GT 500 (1968) 67
FORD MUSTANG FASTBACK (1968) 67
    FASTBACK BOSS 302 (1970) 115
    FASTBACK BULLITT (1968) 67
    FASTBACK DAYTONA (1965) 66
    FASTBACK GT 350 (1965) 66
FORD MUSTANG NOTCHBACK (1965 & 1966) 66
FORD RAIL BUS (1939) 22
FORD RANCHERO (1957) 51, 52, 53
FORD ROADSTER (1932) 47
    ROADSTER (1934) 18
    ROADSTER (1936) 20
    ROADSTER MODEL A (1931) 18
FORD SEDAN MODEL A VICTORIA (1930) 17
FORD SEDAN DELIVERY (1935) 19, 21
    SEDAN DELIVERY (1936) 20, 21
    SEDAN DELIVERY (1940) 23
    SEDAN DELIVERY (1948) 28
    SEDAN DELIVERY COURIER (1954) 45, 47, 108
FORD STATION WAGON (1939) 21, 22, 103
    STATION WAGON (1946) 28
    STATION WAGON (1947) 31, 32
    STATION WAGON (1948) 29
    STATION WAGON COUNTRY SQUIRE (1949) 9, 34, 35
    STATION WAGON COUNTRY SQUIRE (1950) 8, 32, 34, 35
    STATION WAGON COUNTRY SQUIRE (1959) 60, 61
    STATION WAGON COUNTRY SQUIRE (1963) 63
    STATION WAGON COUNTRY SQUIRE (1964) 64
    STATION WAGON DEL RIO (1957) 51, 53, 57, 103

STATION WAGON MODEL A (1932) 18
FORD THUNDERBIRD (1954 & 1955) 54
    THUNDERBIRD (1957) 4, 16, 55, 107
    THUNDERBIRD (1958) 16, 55-57, 103
    THUNDERBIRD (1959) 56, 57
    THUNDERBIRD (1960) 57
    THUNDERBIRD (1961) 64
    THUNDERBIRD (1963) 116
    THUNDERBIRD (1965) 65
    THUNDERBIRD (1967) 65
    THUNDERBIRD (1968) 65
    THUNDERBIRD (1969) 65, 66
    TORINO (1968) 67, 68
    TORINO (1970) 68
FORD TRUCK ECONOLINE (1961) 63
    MODEL AA (1931) 18
    PANEL DELIVERY (1939) 22
    PANEL DELIVERY F1 (1952) 43
    PANEL DELIVERY F100 (1955) 47
    PICKUP (1940) 25
    PICKUP (1942) 27
    PICKUP F1 (1948) 30
    PICKUP F100 (1953) 46
    PICKUP TOW TRUCK F100 (1954) 46
    PICKUP TOW TRUCK F100 (1955) 46
FORD TRUCK RANGER F1 (1952) 43
FORD TRUCK UTILITY F1 (1950) 43
FORD TUDOR SEDAN (1937) 21
    SEDAN (1941) 26, 27
    SEDAN (1946) 28
    SEDAN (1947) 28
    SEDAN (1949) 33
    SEDAN CRESTLINER (1950) 8, 35, 38
    SEDAN CRESTLINER (1951) 8, 39
    SEDAN CUSTOM (1950) 8, 15, 33, 35, 37-39
    SEDAN MAINLINE (1956) 50

LINCOLN CONVERTIBLE CAPRI (1953) 5, 9, 10, 75, 76, 79, 114
    CAPRI (1955) 80, 81, 82
LINCOLN CONVERTIBLE CAPRI FIFTIETH ANNIVERSARY (1953) 79
LINCOLN CONVERTIBLE CAPRI SPECIAL KING HUSSEIN (1953) 79
LINCOLN CONVERTIBLE CAPRI SPEEDSTER (1953) 79
LINCOLN CONVERTIBLE CONTINENTAL (1941) 71, 72
    CONTINENTAL (1959) 88
    CONTINENTAL (1960) 88, 89
    CONTINENTAL (1961) 89, 90
    CONTINENTAL (1964) 90
    CONTINENTAL (1965) 90

CONTINENTAL MkII (1957) 86
LINCOLN CONVERTIBLE COSMOPOLITAN (1949) 74
    COSMOPOLITAN (1951) 7, 69, 74, 75, 83
    COSMOPOLITAN PRESIDENTIAL (1949) 73, 74
LINCOLN CONVERTIBLE PHAETON (1929) 70
LINCOLN CONVERTIBLE PREMIERE (1956) 84
LINCOLN COUPÉ CONTINENTAL (1941) 72
    CONTINENTAL (1946) 73
    CONTINENTAL LOEWY (1946) 72
    HARDTOP CAPRI (1952) 7, 69, 75, 77-79, 83, 104
    HARDTOP CAPRI (1953) 75-77, 78
    HARDTOP CAPRI (1955) 7, 9, 69, 79-83, 98
    HARDTOP CONTINENTAL (1960) 88
    HARDTOP CONTINENTAL MkII (1956) 86, 87
    HARDTOP CONTINENTAL MkII (1957) 85, 86
    HARDTOP CONTINENTAL MkIII (1969) 90
    HARDTOP PREMIERE (1956) 84, 111
    ZEPHYR (1938) 71
LINCOLN DREAM CAR FUTURA (1955) 84
LINCOLN ROADSTER (1927) 70
    ROADSTER (1932) 70
    ROADSTER (1927) 70
    ROADSTER (1932) 70
LINCOLN SEDAN (1948) 73
LINCOLN SEDAN CONTINENTAL (1964) 90
    CONTINENTAL CONCEPT (1951) 75
    COSMOPOLITAN (1950) 73
    COSMOPOLITAN (1952) 79
    LWB CONTINENTAL (1941) 72
    PREMIER (1956) 69, 83, 85, 87, 107
    PREMIER (1957) 4, 69, 87
    ZEPHYR (1937) 70
    ZEPHYR (1938) 71
LINCOLN TOWN CAR (1927) 70
    ZEPHYR (1940) 71

MERCURY CONVERTIBLE (1946) 92
    CONVERTIBLE (1950) 93-95
    CONVERTIBLE (1951) 95
    CONVERTIBLE (1954) 95, 96, 107
    CONVERTIBLE (1955) 96-98
    CONVERTIBLE (1956) 98
    CONVERTIBLE (1957) 4, 91, 98, 99, 100, 112
MERCURY COUGAR (1969) 101, 102
MERCURY COUPÉ (1939) 91, 92
    COUPÉ (1949) 94
    COUPÉ (1950) 93
    COUPÉ HARDTOP (1955) 96-98
    COUPÉ HARDTOP (1956) 11
    COUPÉ HARDTOP (1957) 9, 91, 98-100, 112
    COUPÉ HARDTOP (1964) 101
    COUPÉ HARDTOP SUN VALLEY (1954) 95, 96, 113
    COUPÉ HARDTOP SUN VALLEY (1955) 6, 96-98
MERCURY CYCLONE (1966) 102
    CYCLONE (1968) 101, 102
MERCURY STATION WAGON (1959) 100

PEOPLE/COMPANIES
A&S MODELS 16, 104, 111
ABC MODELS 10, 92
AMERICAN MODELS 113
AMERICAN WHEELS: A REFERENCE 9, 109
AMR 10, 11
AMT MODELS 44
ARMBRUSTER, DICK 76, 114
ARNOLD, BRUCE 12, 13, 34, 44, 63, 65, 68, 76, 104, 105, 107, 109, 112
ASBURY, LLOYD 114
ASHTON MODELS 104
AUTO BUFF MODELS 8, 14, 15, 104, 114
AUTO REPLICAS 8, 115

BAUDET, DENIS 115
BBR MODELS 9, 69, 75, 78, 104, 105

BELGIUM TRUCKS/JUPITER 104, 105
BERKSHIRE VALLEY MODELS 14
BRIANZA, CARLO 78
BRIGGS, RICHARD 99, 112
BROOKLIN COLLECTORS CLUB UK 105
BROOKLIN MODELS 8, 9, 14-16, 51, 64, 69, 73, 84, 85, 88, 91-93, 99, 105, 106, 109, 110
BROSSI, MARCEL 11
BROWNE, DICK 4 105
BRUCE ARNOLD MODELS 10, 103
BUBY, CARLOS 106

CANADIAN TOY COLLECTORS' SOCIETY (CTCS) 105
CCC MODELS 10, 15
CENTURY MODELS 17, 89
COLUZZI, GIANSANTE 115
COLLECTOR CASE MODELS 20
COLLECTORS' CLASSICS MODELS 15, 44, 69, 95, 106, 107
CONQUEST MODELS 9, 16, 55, 64, 73, 107, 108
CORGI TOYS 51, 107, 109

DANBURY MINT 69
DANINDEN, GERARD 115
DESIGN STUDIO MODELS 44, 91, 113, 116
DICKSON, JOEL 111
DIECAST ZONE 110, 114
DINKY TOYS 107, 109
DU CROSS, GRAHAM 111
DUNCAN, ALISTAIR 16, 103
DUNCAN, SALLY 16, 103
DURHAM CLASSICS 9, 14-16, 51, 76, 91, 108

ECMA 15, 110
ENCHANTMENT LAND COACHBUILDERS (ELC) 9, 16, 64, 69, 70, 93, 109, 110

FA. DAIMLER HOUSE 17, 69, 84, 107, 108
FORTY-THIRD AVENUE (FTA) MODELS 9, 92, 111
FORUM 43 5
FRANKLIN MINT 16
FROBLY MODELS 91, 93, 110

GOLDVARG COLLECTION MODELS 10, 91, 95, 110
GOLDVARG, MARIANA 110
GOLDVARG, SERGIO 110
GREAT AMERICAN DREAM MACHINES 103

HAGLEY, NICK 112
HALL, JOHN 105, 109
HECO MODELS 17
HEITECH MODELS 110
HIGHWAY TRAVELERS MODELS 10

ILLUSTRA MODELS 17, 111

JPS MODELS, 10

K&D AUTOMOBILIA MODELS 10, 17, 111
KAGER MODELS 15
KENNA, PETER 105
KIRKEL, BUZ 107
KLARWASSER, GERHARD 104

LANG, GUNTER 116
LEGENDARY MOTORCARS 9, 69, 70, 88, 89, 111
LESTER, BARRY 104

MA SCALE MODELS 17
MADISON MODELS 9, 84, 107, 108
MARQUE ONE MODELS 16, 111
MESQUITE MODELS 93
MIDLANTIC MODELS 103, 111, 112
MIKANSUE MODELS 8
MILESTONE MINIATURES 9, 14, 16, 17, 64, 92, 101, 111

MINI MARQUE 10, 111
MINI MARQUE '43' MODELS 10, 14, 16, 88, 89, 92, 99, 104, 112
MINICHAMPS MODELS 85, 93, 101, 111, 117
MODEL AUTO REVIEW 4, 76, 115
MODELEX 100
MOORHOUSE, GEOFF 115
MOTOR CITY USA MODELS 5-8, 10, 11, 14, 15, 33, 69, 73, 76, 85, 91, 95, 109, 110, 113, 116
MURRAY, MIKE 112

NOSTALGIC MINIATURES 8, 14, 16, 17, 44, 114
NOVAK, ALAN 113
NYE, CLIVE 112

OAKLAND MODELS 15, 44, 114
OVERY, STEVE 112

PAOLUCCI, DEAN 4
PARKER, NIGEL 105
PARRILL, GENE 76, 114
PICKERING, IAN 105, 112
PONT, GEORGES 115
PRECISION MINIATURES MODELS 8, 17, 69, 76, 114
PROVENCE MOULAGE MODELS 8, 15

RETTIG, JERRY 4, 93, 109
REXTOYS MODELS 115
RICHARD CARLSON PRODUCTS 109
RICHARDSON, MIKE 8
RICHARDSON, SUE 8
RIO 69, 109
ROBERTS, JOHN 11, 12
RUF, ANDRE-MARIE 10, 11

SAN FRANCISCO BAY BROOKLIN CLUB (SFBBC) 105
SCALE MODEL TECHNICAL SERVICES (SMTS) 9, 10, 16, 17, 107, 108
SHROCK BROTHERS 103
SKYLINE MODELS 91, 93, 110, 116
SMITH, ALAN 115
SOLIDO 109
SPOT-ON 107
STARTER MODELS 17
STEPHENS, JOYCE 117
STEPHENS, MIKE 4, 67, 116, 117
STEWART, JULIAN 109, 114
STEWART, MARGARET 109
STYLING MODELS 104
SUN MOTOR COMPANY 115

THOMAS, ANDREW 4
TIN WIZARD MODELS 10, 17, 61, 64, 93, 110, 116, 117
TOYS FOR COLLECTORS MODELS (TFC) 10, 64, 92, 101, 111, 116
TRAX MODELS 16
TRON MODELS 10

US MODEL MINT 15
USA MODELS 91, 113

VAN ASTEN, HENK 107
VICTORY MODELS 10, 103

WARD, ROD 4, 76, 115
WESTERN MODELS 8, 14, 15, 16, 64, 69, 71, 75, 110, 116, 117
WOLTER, THOMAS 116
WWW.AMR-MODELCARS.COM 11
WWW.DIECAST.ORG 5
WWW.LINCOLNDOWNUNDER.COM 78

ZAUGG, JÖRG 116, 117
ZAUGG MODELS 8, 16, 17, 91, 92, 93, 101, 114, 116, 117

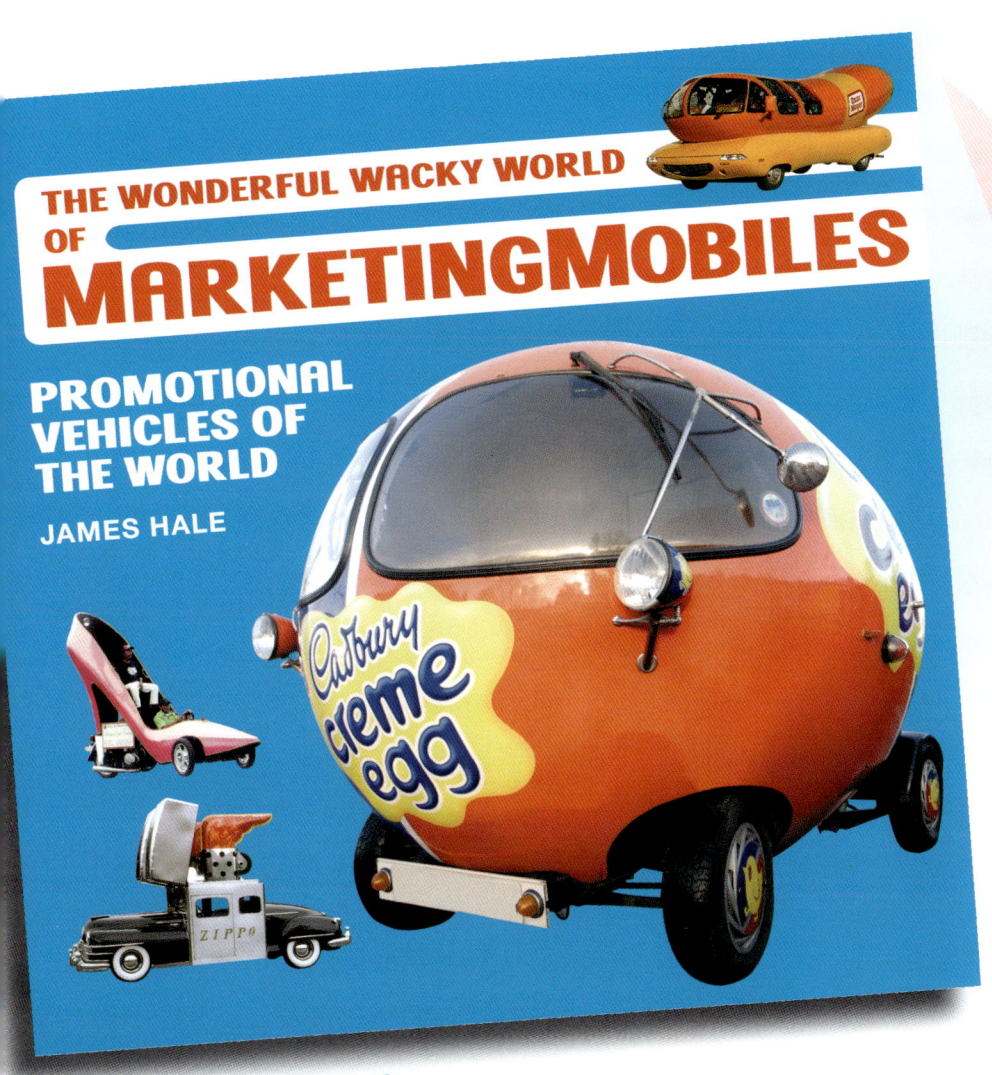

MORE GREAT VELOCE BOOKS!

p&p extra; please call 01305 260068 for rates
www.velocebooks.com

ISBN 1904788963 • £24.99

ISBN 1904788971 • £24.99

p&p extra; please call 01305 260068 for rates
www.velocebooks.com

ISBN 190370667X • £29.99

ISBN 19904788866 • £19.99

ISBN 1904788769 • £19.99

p&p extra; please call 01305 260068 for rates
www.velocebooks.com